I0818380

Praise for Dan Sullivan and John Bowen

"I've spent my career proving that exponential thinking outperforms linear thinking. Sullivan and Bowen have applied that principle to entrepreneurship with research-backed precision. Their Greater Multipliers Study reveals what I've observed: the entrepreneurs who create the most value don't work harder—they architect systems, platforms, and ecosystems that scale automatically. Essential reading for any founder ready to think 100x."

— Peter H. Diamandis, MD, founder & chairman, XPRIZE and Abundance360; *New York Times* best-selling author of *Abundance*, *BOLD*, and *We Are As Gods*

"For twenty years, I've watched Genius Network prove what Sullivan and Bowen spell out in this book: the entrepreneurs who win the biggest game aren't trying to beat everyone—they're building ecosystems where everyone multiplies. The shift from being indispensable to building platforms that scale genius? That's not just smart business, it's the only way to create real freedom AND impact. This book gives you the research and the road map to make that shift."

— Joe Polish, founder of Genius Network®

"The greatest wealth transfer in history is underway. Sullivan and Bowen show entrepreneurs how to architect businesses that capture it—and create a lasting legacy in the process."

— David Bach, 10x *New York Times* best-selling author of *The Automatic Millionaire* and *Smart Women Finish Rich*

"In the second half of life, we stop asking 'How do I do more?' and start asking 'How do I matter more?' This book answers that question for entrepreneurs."

— Chip Conley, founder, Modern Elder Academy; *New York Times* best-selling author

"After interviewing thousands of ultra-wealthy entrepreneurs, a clear pattern emerges: those who built lasting wealth shifted from constantly optimizing to designing their legacies. Sullivan and Bowen capture this mindset and make it accessible to entrepreneurs ready to think bigger."

— Russ Alan Prince, president of R.A. Prince & Associates; leading authority on ultra-high-net-worth families

"100x really is easier than 2x when you stop doing everything yourself. The Greater Game *shows entrepreneurs how to turn their expertise into scalable platforms and self-managing teams so impact grows while time freedom expands. Essential reading for anyone ready to build an empire—not just a business."*

— JJ Virgin, *New York Times* best-selling author; 2x Inc. 5000 founder, Reignite Wellness & Health Business Growth Collective

"John Bowen and Dan Sullivan are entrepreneurs who have each spent their careers studying and advising other successful entrepreneurs on how to take their businesses to the next level. This book distills the knowledge they have acquired over more than three decades and empowers business owners to create a legacy built on sustainable enterprise value."

— Evan Simonoff, editor-in-chief, *Financial Advisor Magazine*

"Most entrepreneurs don't build businesses. They build beautiful cages. I've both seen it and lived it firsthand. Dan Sullivan and John Bowen don't just name the trap, they hand you the keys out."

— Jayson Gaignard, co-founder of MMT

"Most entrepreneurs optimize their way to a ceiling. The Greater Game *shows how to architect beyond it—grounded in research, real stories, and a proven framework."*

— Simon Bowen, founder & CEO, The Models Method

"Bowen and Sullivan nailed it. The concept of 'architect' resonates! The Greater Game *guides transformation and impact. It doesn't just move the needle, it resets the clock! Powerful insights and action plan. Want results . . . embrace this vision!"*

— Jim Tracy, wealth management senior executive

THE GREATER GAME

ALSO BY DAN SULLIVAN

With Dr. Benjamin Hardy

The Gap and The Gain: The High Achievers' Guide to Happiness, Confidence, and Success

Who Not How: The Formula to Achieve Bigger Goals Through Accelerating Teamwork

10x Is Easier Than 2x: How World-Class Entrepreneurs Achieve More by Doing Less

All of the above are available at your local bookstore,
or may be ordered by visiting:

Hay House USA: www.hayhouse.com®
Hay House Australia: www.hayhouse.com.au
Hay House UK: www.hayhouse.co.uk
Hay House India: www.hayhouse.co.in

THE GREATER GAME

Your 100x Blueprint for Exponential Growth, Freedom, and Legacy

Why Tomorrow's Winners Refuse To Play Today's Game

DAN SULLIVAN
Founder of Strategic Coach

JOHN BOWEN
Founder of CEG Elevate Group

HAY HOUSE LLC
Carlsbad, California • New York City
London • Sydney • New Delhi

Published in the United States by: Hay House LLC, www.hayhouse.com®
P.O. Box 5100, Carlsbad, CA, 92018-5100

Project editor: Melody Guy • *Interior design:* Lisa Vega

Hardcover ISBN: 979-8-3186-0426-3
E-book ISBN: 979-8-3186-0427-0
Audiobook ISBN: 979-8-3186-0428-7

1st Printing

Printed in the United States of America

This product uses responsibly sourced papers, including recycled materials and materials from other controlled sources.

The authorized representative in the EU for product safety and compliance is Penguin Random House Ireland, Morrison Chambers, 32 Nassau Street, Dublin D02 YH68, Ireland. https://eu-contact.penguin.ie

CONTENTS

CONTENTS

INTRODUCTION

THE 18-MONTH WINDOW AND THE GREATER GAME

You've built something impressive:

- Revenue: $20 million and growing steadily
- Team: 60 solid people
- Industry standing: respected, even envied

So why does success feel like drowning in slow motion?

Three acquisition announcements landed this week. Competitors selling for 8x, 12x, even 15x earnings before interest, taxes, depreciation and amortization (EBITDA). The last one—someone you dismissed five years ago—just sold to a strategic buyer using AI to revolutionize the game you invented.

You've won the wrong game.

The difference between you and them: They stopped optimizing operations and started architecting ecosystems. They transformed their expertise into intellectual property (IP) that multiplies without them, while yours dies without your presence.

Here's what's keeping you awake: You've won the wrong game.

Last week, your 14-year-old daughter asked you, "What exactly do you do that's so important you miss my games?" You gave her a speech about building a legacy—but even as you said it, you knew it was hollow. The truth you couldn't admit: You're solving the same problems you solved five years ago, just with bigger numbers.

You've discovered the secret that destroys most successful entrepreneurs: Every system that got you here is optimized for a game that's coming to an end. Every strength that built your fortune is becoming irrelevant.

You are not burned out. You are misaligned. You haven't misplayed the game—you've outgrown the field.

Here's the question that changes everything: What if the exhaustion you feel isn't from poor execution but from perfect execution of an outdated strategy?

THE 5.4% INSIGHT: THE SHIFT FROM OPTIMIZATION TO ARCHITECTURE

Our Greater Multipliers Study, which surveyed 1,016 entrepreneurs,[1] revealed that only 5.4% operate with what we call an exponential architecture—a fundamentally different approach to growth.

The remaining 94.6% optimize within existing constraints—working harder, faster, and longer. They're fighting the physics of their current model.

The 5.4% operate from an entirely different paradigm. They don't just think bigger; they architect differently. They understand the central paradox of the Greater Game:

[1] Findings cited as Greater Multipliers Study (n=1016) and Entrepreneurial Pulse reflect proprietary surveys conducted by CEG Insights in 2025.

100X IS EASIER THAN 2X

When you aim for 2x growth, you optimize. It's exhausting.

When you aim for 100x, optimization is impossible. You are forced to abandon your current model and architect something entirely new. You build platforms, not products. You design ecosystems, not organizations. You transform competitors into multipliers.

This architectural approach requires less effort over time because the systems scale up automatically.

Consider the evidence:

- Roderick Walker (Chapter 1) shifted from managing two health care locations in 70 hours a week to overseeing 14 locations in 25 hours by architecting an operational platform.
- Dale Wills (Chapter 5) transformed his biggest threat (banks) into his most incredible multiplier, achieving 10x growth during a recession.
- Mike Wandler (Chapter 6) reduced his headcount from 600 to 250 while doubling revenue—by shifting from managing people to multiplying genius.

They didn't work harder. They architected differently.

THE 18-MONTH WINDOW THAT CHANGES EVERYTHING

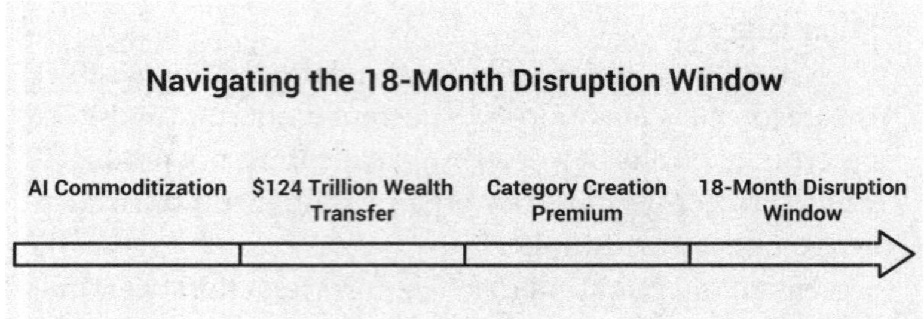

While you're reading this Introduction, three forces are converging that make this architectural shift mandatory. You have 18 months before these forces make your current game obsolete.

1. AI Is Commoditizing Excellence

AI is rapidly collapsing execution advantages. McKinsey[2] research indicates that while investment in AI is broad, most companies remain immature in capturing its value. The winners are rewiring workflows, governance, and talent. Your operational excellence? Table stakes. Your execution advantage? Increasingly automated. In this environment, vision and architecture become the only defensible moats.

2. The $124 Trillion Wealth Transfer

The most significant generational wealth transfer in history—an estimated $124 trillion through 2048 (Cerulli Associates, 2025 estimates)—is underway. They're funding moonshots, not maintenance. If your vision doesn't excite a 35-year-old with $50 million to deploy, you're already obsolete.

---

2 McKinsey & Company, "The State of AI in 2025: How Organizations Are Rewiring to Capture Value," McKinsey Global Survey, January 2025.

3. The Category Creation Premium

The market no longer rewards being better—it rewards being different. Category creators (like Airbnb, Stripe, and Salesforce) command premium valuation multiples. Category competitors (the optimizers) often settle for 3–5x.

The comfortable truth? You could maintain your current success for another year. While you're optimizing your present, someone is architecting your replacement.

WHO THIS BOOK IS REALLY FOR (AND WHO SHOULD CLOSE IT NOW)

Let's be brutally clear: This book will transform the right reader and disappoint everyone else.

This book IS for you if:

- You've achieved success, but you are starved for significance.
- You've built a thriving business, but you own a job, not an asset.
- You know your current ceiling is actually your future floor.
- You are ready to shift from being the indispensable bottleneck to the invincible architect.

This book will DISAPPOINT you if you still believe

- Sixty-hour workweeks are the price of success
- Linear growth (10% annually) is exciting
- Your expertise is too complex to package into IP
- Business must be a zero-sum game

If you're looking for your first million, we'll frustrate you. If you're protecting your tenth million while architecting your hundredth million in impact, keep reading.

TWO COLLAPSES THAT BECAME CATALYSTS

We (Dan Sullivan and John Bowen) didn't discover the Greater Game in a boardroom. We found it through catastrophic failure. We learned the hard way that success without exponential architecture is a house of cards.

JOHN'S COLLAPSE: WHEN OPTIMIZATION FAILS

May 5, 1975, junior year of college. I (John) was being groomed to take over our family's 400-employee foundry—our legacy, our identity.

Then the phone rang. "John, I have some tough news. The foundry is going under. Your mother and I are getting divorced."

I was stunned. Two generations of "perfect systems" had optimized their way to obsolescence. My parents had won yesterday's game so completely that they never saw tomorrow's game beginning. They had processes but no multipliers. They had structure but no transformation.

That collapse forced me to recognize the fatal flaw of the 94.6% game: Optimization without architecture leads to inevitable failure. It led me to dedicate my life to helping entrepreneurs build proper security and invincibility (Chapter 2).

DAN'S CATALYST: FROM BANKRUPTCY TO BREAKTHROUGH

August 15, 1978. Divorced and bankrupt—on the same day. Everything I (Dan) had built was gone.

But something curious happened. Despite losing everything, clients continued to want to work with me. They valued the frameworks and thinking tools I had created.

In that dark space, I realized I had been building something far more potent than I understood: intellectual property (Chapter 4). I had unconsciously created multipliers.

Strategic Coach wasn't born from inspiration. It was born from collapse—and the recognition that the actual value wasn't my time but my architecture. From that insight, I developed the frameworks that would transform over 25,000 entrepreneurs through Strategic Coach.

OUR COMBINED DISCOVERY: THE GREATER GAME

Decades later, our combined journey—Dan's and John's—revealed the blueprint for exponential growth. It's not about avoiding collapse; it's about using strategic architecture to turn every challenge into a catalyst for growth.

You don't have to wait for a collapse to force recognition. You can make the shift strategically, deliberately, and exponentially.

THE ARCHITECTURE OF EXPONENTIAL IMPACT: THE GREATER GAME PYRAMID

The Greater Game is played across four stages, powered by 10 multipliers. This is the architecture that the 5.4% use to achieve 100x results.

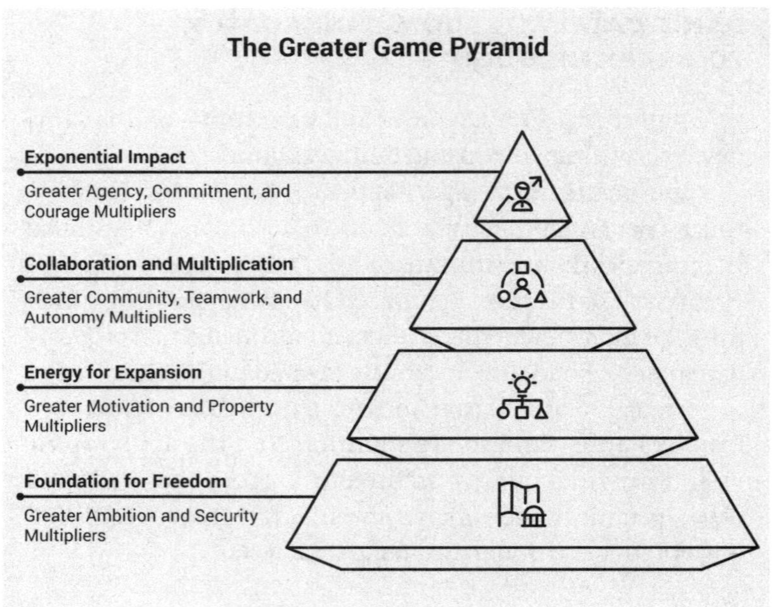

THE 10 MULTIPLIERS: YOUR BLUEPRINT FOR THE 100X FUTURE

This book is the architectural blueprint for implementing these 10 multipliers, systematically transforming your business from an optimization machine into an exponential ecosystem.

STAGE 1: FOUNDATION FOR FREEDOM

This stage lays the unshakable foundation that enables 100x growth.

- **Chapter 1: Greater Ambition—Engineering Your 100x Future.** This is the shift from 2x optimization to 100x architecture. You'll learn why 56.4% of the 5.4% embed long-term vision into every decision—compared to just 14.2% of other entrepreneurs—and how visionaries like Paul VanDuyne used this 25-year thinking to achieve 12x growth after age 65.

- **Chapter 2: Greater Security—the Foundation That Makes Everything Possible.** The paradox is that the most aggressive entrepreneurs are the most protected. You'll learn to architect invincibility through coordinated wealth orchestration, turning your disconnected advisors into a cohesive team and eliminating the coordination gaps that affect 94.6% of clients.

STAGE 2: ENERGY FOR EXPANSION

This stage transforms your internal genius into scalable assets that multiply without you.

- **Chapter 3: Greater Motivation—Engineering Your Self-Generating Success Engine.** This is the shift from the external depletion cycle to internal generation. You'll learn David Reiling's Mission x Margin formula, which powered his bank from $14 million to $2.5 billion by focusing on the emotional paycheck.
- **Chapter 4: Greater Property—Your Genius Becomes Your Empire.** This tells you how to escape the expertise trap by transforming your brilliance into scalable intellectual property

(IP). You'll see how Keegan Caldwell utilized IP architecture to achieve a 341% growth rate while reducing his work hours by 60%.

STAGE 3: COLLABORATION AND MULTIPLICATION

This stage moves you from individual excellence to exponential ecosystems, achieving scale through strategic partnerships and self-managing teams.

- **Chapter 5: Greater Community—Your Competition Becomes Your Multiplier.** This is the shift from zero-sum competition to positive-sum ecosystem creation. You'll learn about the architecture behind free-zone collaborations, where adversaries become amplifiers, as demonstrated by Dale Wills, who achieved 10x growth during a recession.
- **Chapter 6: Greater Teamwork—from Managing People to Multiplying Genius.** This is the crucial shift from delegation to empowerment. You'll discover how to build self-managing teams that eliminate founder dependency (the "indispensability discount") and unlock 10–15x valuation multiples.
- **Chapter 7: Greater Autonomy—from Indispensable to Invincible.** This is the ultimate liberation. You'll learn how to engineer your freedom, making your presence optional while your impact becomes exponential, as demonstrated by Gino Wickman, whose EOS (Entrepreneurial Operating System) now transforms more than

300,000 companies without his involvement, and Evan Ryan, who traveled 300 days while his company grew 5x (the absence multiplier).

STAGE 4: EXPONENTIAL IMPACT

This stage leverages your freedom to create transformative change, moving from reacting to markets to making them.

- **Chapter 8: Greater Agency—from Reacting to Creating Markets.** This is the discipline of category design. You'll learn how entrepreneurs like Carter Froelich and Brian Chesky (Airbnb) overcame conventional barriers and forced entire industries to adapt to their vision.
- **Chapter 9: Greater Commitment—the Compound Effect of Strategic Stubbornness.** This is the power of maintaining vision immutability while ensuring tactical flexibility. You'll learn how Steven Neuner's 20-year commitment enabled him to build his second company in just 3 years—what had taken 15 years the first time.
- **Chapter 10: Greater Courage—Your Fear Is Your Compass.** This is the final multiplier. While only 2.3% of the 94.6% harness fear of falling behind as motivation, 9.1% of the 5.4% don't eliminate fear; they weaponize it. You'll learn how to transform terror into exponential fuel, as demonstrated by Jensen Huang's more than $4 trillion market cap (as of September 2025) bet on AI.

THE PROMISE: THE QUANTIFIABLE IMPACT OF THE GREATER GAME

This isn't just theory. The shift from optimization to architecture has a profound impact on enterprise value and personal freedom.

THE VALUATION EVIDENCE: THE ARCHITECTURE PREMIUM

The market doesn't reward effort; it rewards architecture.

- **The optimization trap (the 94.6%):** 3–5x EBITDA; founder-dependent, linear growth, high exhaustion
- **The exponential architecture (the 5.4%):** premium multiples (often 15x+); IP-driven, ecosystem-focused, self-managing, high-energy

On a $4 million EBITDA business, that's the difference between a $16 million exit and an $80+ million exit. Your current strategy is costing you tens of millions of dollars.

THE FREEDOM EVIDENCE: THE LIFE INTEGRATION

But the fundamental transformation isn't in the numbers. It's in the lives.

- John Kissell (Chapter 4): His business ran itself—and grew—during a life-threatening hospitalization, proving the resilience of his architecture.

- Kent Pilcher (Chapter 6): He went from 14 vacation days to 100+ days for family and strategic thinking.
- Steven Neuner (Chapter 9): He takes 150+ free days annually while achieving 100% year-over-year growth.

The Greater Game isn't about work-life balance. It's about life integration, where your business creates you rather than consumes you.

YOUR STRATEGIC RECOGNITION AND THE DASHBOARD

Here's what we discovered through our collapses: Success creates strategic by-products—patterns, systems, wisdom—that most entrepreneurs never recognize or capture. These are your hidden multipliers.

This book doesn't teach you something entirely new—it helps you recognize, name, and multiply what you've already created.

To make this transformation systematic, we've built an exclusive companion tool for readers: the **Greater Game Dashboard** (visit TheGreaterGameDashboard.com or scan the QR code below). This free online assessment takes 15 minutes and reveals your GMI Score—a composite metric measuring your exponential growth potential across all 10

Multipliers. At the end of each chapter, you'll complete a Multiplier Activation exercise and Scorecard. Input your results into the dashboard to unlock your personalized Command Center—showing exactly where you stand, how you compare to the top 5.4%, and your three highest-leverage moves right now.

The dashboard provides:

- **The Greater Multipliers Index (GMI):** your composite metric tracking your journey to a 100x future
- **The Entrepreneurial Pulse:** benchmarking your progress against the top 5.4% of performers identified in our monthly proprietary research
- **The Growth Playbook:** personalized strategies identifying your highest-leverage path forward—whether that's Strategic Coach Acceleration (execution frameworks and founder dependence solutions) or Virtual Family Office (VFO) Second Opinion (wealth complexity and concentration risk solutions)

This isn't just a book; it's an integrated system for transformation.

THE CHOICE THAT DEFINES EVERYTHING

Tomorrow morning, you'll wake up to the same business, the same team, and the same challenges. But you now face a choice the 94.6% don't know exists:

Path A: the optimization trap: Continue perfecting your current game. Work harder. Accept exhaustion as the price of success. Settle for 3–5x multiples.

Path B: the multiplication path: Shift from optimization to architecture. Build ecosystems, IP, and self-managing teams. Achieve exponential impact and premium multiples.

Optimization builds your success. Multiplication builds your legacy.

Optimization got you here. Multiplication gets you free.

THE ONLY QUESTION THAT MATTERS

Your daughter's question still hangs in the air: What exactly do you do that's so important you miss her games?

What if, by the time you finish this book, you had an answer that made both of you proud?

The 94.6% will read this and return to optimization—still unable to answer her question.

The 5.4% will recognize what's already working, multiply it, and finally have an answer that makes you both proud.

Which will you choose?

Turn the page. Chapter 1 marks the beginning of your transformation from unconscious excellence to strategic architecture.

Welcome to the 5.4%. Welcome to the Greater Game.

That restless feeling that brought you here? This page is your launchpad. Let's begin.

STAGE 1

FOUNDATION FOR FREEDOM

GREATER AMBITION + GREATER SECURITY

Before you can multiply, you must stabilize. Before you can scale, you must secure. Before you can transform an industry, you must transform your foundation.

THE TRUTH ABOUT YOUR NEXT LEVEL

Right now, at this exact moment, you're standing on quicksand disguised as solid ground.

Your business is thriving. Your reputation is solid. Your bank account is healthy. Yet something fundamental is missing—the foundation that would let you build exponentially without fear of collapse.

You've been trying to solve a multiplication problem with addition tools—trying to achieve 100x results with 2x thinking and trying to build a skyscraper on a foundation designed for a suburban home.

Here's what the 5.4% discovered that the 94.6% never will: Exponential growth doesn't start with aggressive expansion. It begins with an unshakable foundation.

WHY EVERY BREAKTHROUGH BEGINS HERE

Think about the entrepreneurs you've just met in the Introduction:

- Roderick Walker, who would grow from 2 health care locations to 14 while cutting his hours from 70 to 25, didn't rush to scale—he built an operational platform first.
- Paul VanDuyne didn't just acquire companies—he first engineered a 25-year vision.
- David Reiling married 'do well, do good'—then let community needs shape the systems.

They all understood: **You can't build a billion-dollar future on a million-dollar foundation.**

Stage 1 isn't about slowing down. It's about building the platform that makes everything else possible. It's the difference between:

- Running faster vs. building a vehicle
- Working harder vs. creating systems
- Managing risk vs. engineering it out
- Having ambition vs. architecting it

THE TWO PILLARS THAT CHANGE EVERYTHING

Greater ambition (Chapter 1) isn't dreaming bigger—it's seeing the invisible architecture of exponential growth. It's the recognition that 100x is actually easier than 2x because it forces complete reimagination rather than incremental improvement. Chapter 1 will show you how Walker, VanDuyne, and Cotten discovered this paradox and rode it to transformation.

Greater security (Chapter 2) isn't about protection—it's about permission. It's the systematic elimination of concentration risk that allows you to make bold moves without existential fear. Chapter 2 reveals how Akerley turned $500,000 into $80 million in revenue and, ultimately, to a nine-figure exit to a Fortune 500 company, and Lake turned $5,000 into $1.1 billion by building invincibility first, then aggression.

Together, they create something the 94.6% never achieve: **freedom to play offense with a defense that's already won.**

THE PARADOX OF PROTECTED AGGRESSION

Here's what keeps most entrepreneurs trapped: They believe they must choose between security and growth. Between protection and expansion. Between stability and transformation.

The 5.4% discovered the opposite is true:

- The most aggressive entrepreneurs are the most protected.
- The fastest growers have the strongest foundations.
- The most significant risk-takers have eliminated the most risks.
- The boldest visionaries have the most bulletproof systems.

When you complete Stage 1, you won't just have a business. You'll have:

- A 25-year vision that makes today's problems irrelevant
- Systematic protection that makes failure impossible

- Diversified architecture that eliminates concentration risk
- Strategic clarity that transforms chaos into competitive advantage

WHAT HAPPENS WHEN YOU SKIP THIS STAGE

We've watched hundreds of entrepreneurs attempt to jump straight to multiplication without a solid foundation. They all hit the same walls:

- Growth creates complexity that eventually implodes.
- Success amplifies vulnerabilities until they crack.
- Expansion without architecture becomes expensive chaos.
- Ambition without security becomes reckless gambling.

You've probably seen it yourself—the competitor who grew fast and flamed out, the industry leader who seemed invincible until they weren't, or the entrepreneur who had everything until one decision destroyed it all.

They skipped Stage 1. Don't be them.

WHAT STAGE 1 WILL GIVE YOU

By the time you finish Stage 1, you'll have:

1. A 25-year vision that energizes rather than exhausts

2. The Security Stack that protects while multiplying
3. Recognition of the multipliers you've already been creating
4. The blueprint for systematic invincibility
5. Proof that 100x is easier than 2x

But more importantly, you'll have something the 94.6% never achieve: **The foundation that makes everything else not just possible but inevitable.**

THE CHOICE BEFORE YOU TURN THIS PAGE

You can read Chapter 1 as inspiration—another set of success stories to admire from a distance.

Or you can read it as architecture—the blueprint for your own transformation from exhausted excellence to exponential freedom.

The entrepreneurs you're about to meet weren't exceptional. They weren't chosen. They weren't lucky.

They just recognized that the foundation determines the future. That security enables aggression. That vision without structure is a hallucination.

Stage 1 isn't the exciting part. It's not the sexy part. It's not the part that makes headlines.

It's just the part that makes everything else possible.

Turn the page. Your foundation—and your freedom—await.

CHAPTER 1

GREATER AMBITION—ENGINEERING YOUR 100X FUTURE

While others celebrate reaching the summit,
you're already engineering the next mountain.

THE MONDAY MORNING PARADOX

Every entrepreneur knows this moment: Monday morning, when the workweek stretches ahead and you're forced to confront not just what you're doing, but why. The paradox? Every metric shows success—revenue up, team solid, competitors respectful. Yet the game feels too small. Success without significance.

This restlessness is universal among breakthrough entrepreneurs. When Sam Walton had 500 successful stores, he was already planning 5,000 more. When Steve Jobs returned to Apple in 1997, he wasn't thinking about saving the company—he was imagining putting 1,000 songs in your pocket. The entrepreneurs who reshape industries share this trait:

They are allergic to arrival. Success makes them more ambitious, not less. They instinctively understand that the most significant risk isn't failure—it's stagnation.

That restlessness you're feeling? It's not exhaustion—it's expansion trying to break through. It's the recognition that your current ceiling is actually your future floor. You're standing at the first stage of the Greater Game Pyramid, where greater ambition becomes the foundation for everything that follows.

THE 5.4% WHO PLAY DIFFERENTLY

Our Greater Multipliers Study, which surveyed 1,016 entrepreneurs, revealed a startling pattern: Only 5.4% operate with what we call greater ambition—a fundamentally different approach where multiplication replaces optimization. (Unless otherwise noted, all statistics in this book are drawn from this study.)

They don't just think bigger; they operate from an entirely different architecture. They share six characteristics that enable their exponential results:

THE EXPONENTIAL RESULTS:

- **Visionary** leaders who see beyond linear growth
- **Resilient** leaders who transform setbacks into data
- **Growth-oriented** minds where improvement is the operating system
- **Action-oriented** executors who build while others debate

- **Confident** believers in their ability to execute
- **Resourceful** creators who thrive despite constraints

The data reveals a causal link: Among entrepreneurs generating $50 million or more, 28.1% maintain an unwavering 25-year vision commitment, compared to only 11.3% of those under $10 million. The pattern is unmistakable: Wealth doesn't just follow ambition; it requires it.

THE SUCCESS DELUSION

Your success has become your liability. It creates a gravitational pull toward protection rather than progression. The systems that got you here are optimized for a game that's ending.

The comfortable truth? You could maintain your current success for another decade. The uncomfortable truth? While you're optimizing your present, someone is architecting your replacement.

Consider Blockbuster in 2004: 9,000 stores, $5.9 billion in revenue, 84,000 employees. They were optimizing late fees while Netflix was eliminating stores. Their operational excellence became their epitaph. They optimized their way to obsolescence.

THE 18-MONTH DISRUPTION WINDOW

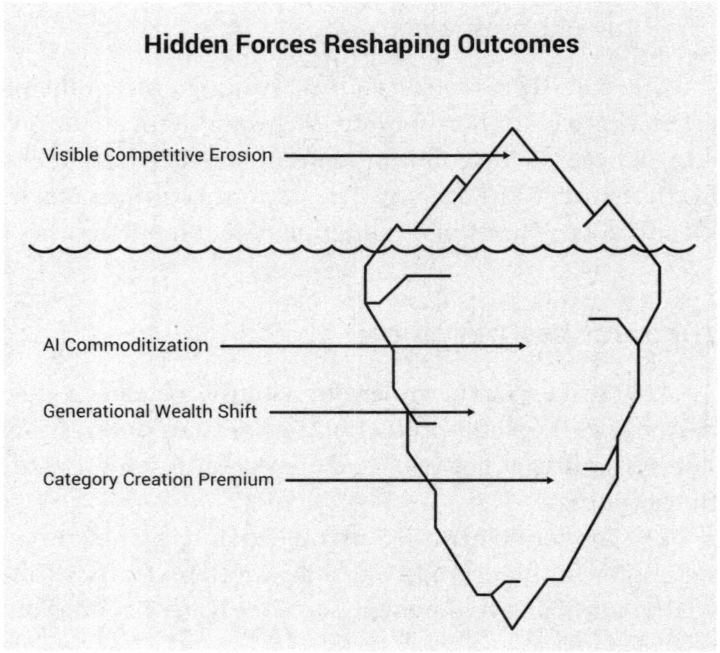

As we established in the Introduction, three forces are converging that will determine the winners of the next decade. Let's explore what each means for your business specifically.

1. AI Commoditizing Excellence

AI is rapidly collapsing execution advantages. McKinsey research indicates that the gap is widening between AI leaders and laggards. As mentioned earlier: Your operational excellence? Table stakes. Your customer service edge? Increasingly automated. Your data analysis advantage? Every competitor will have access to it by 2027.

The only remaining moat is vision—the ability to see and create what doesn't yet exist. If you are competing on execution, you have already lost.

2. The Generational Wealth Transfer

An estimated $124 trillion through 2048 (Cerulli Associates, 2025 estimates) to younger generations. This new class of capital allocators doesn't want to preserve; they want to transform. They're funding moonshots, not maintenance. If your vision doesn't excite a 35-year-old with $50 million to deploy, you're already obsolete.

3. The Category Creation Premium

Recent exits tell the story: Category creators (Uber, Airbnb, Tesla) command premium valuation multiples. Category competitors often settle for 3–5x. The market no longer rewards being better—it rewards being different. It rewards architecture, not optimization.

THE PARADOX OF THE GREATER GAME: 100X IS EASIER THAN 2X

Here is the central paradox that defines the 5.4%: When you aim for 2x growth, you optimize your current systems. You work harder, faster, and longer within the existing constraints. It's exhausting because you are fighting the physics of your current model.

When you aim for 100x, optimization is impossible. You are forced to abandon your current model and architect something entirely new. You build platforms, not products. You design ecosystems, not organizations. This architectural approach requires less effort over time because the systems scale up automatically.

FOUR TRANSFORMATIONS THAT DEFINE GREATER AMBITION

RODERICK WALKER: WHEN SYSTEMS BECOME PLATFORMS

In 2015, Roderick Walker ran two locations of his Oregon health care services company, Tavros Care. He worked 70-hour weeks, believing that more complex work would yield bigger results—classic 94.6% thinking: linear growth through sacrificial effort.

Walker's transformation began when he joined mastermind groups, where extraordinary thinking became normalized. "I was inspired by the highly successful people around me and decided that's where I should be too," Walker says.

But inspiration without architecture is just aspiration. Walker's breakthrough came when he stopped asking "How can I work harder?" and started asking "How can I architect a system where my effort is irrelevant?" He shifted from operator to architect.

He developed what became his operational excellence framework:

- Created 147 detailed operational checklists covering every scenario
- Built real-time performance dashboards tracking 12 key performance indicators (KPIs)
- Standardized the location launch process

The quantified transformation tells the story:

- **Revenue growth**: 650% revenue growth over a 7-year period

- **Locations:** from 2 to 14 (600% growth)
- **Time freedom:** from 70 to 25 hours weekly (64% reduction)
- **Net margins:** from 15% to 24% (60% improvement)

The transformation wasn't just growth—it was liberation. While his competitors still work 70-hour weeks managing two or three locations, Walker oversees 14 locations in 25 hours.

"Every adult care provider in America faces the same operational challenges," Walker realized. "Why are we all solving them separately?"

Now he's building something that transforms his entire industry: a platform that turns competitors into customers. Other providers will license his operational systems, validating his model while paying for the privilege. This is 100x thinking: solving the industry's problem, not just his own.

PAUL VANDUYNE: THE POWER OF 25-YEAR THINKING

At 65, Paul VanDuyne had every reason to coast. As CEO of engineering firm IMEG since 2003, he'd grown it from under 200 to 450 employees. The firm was profitable and stable. His retirement plan was set: a coffee shop with his wife.

Then came the question that changed everything: "What would you accomplish if you had 25 more years to live?"

"That day literally changed everything for me," VanDuyne recalls. "I went from planning lattes in retirement to envisioning IMEG as a billion-dollar platform for engineering excellence. My wife thought I'd lost my mind—until she saw how energized I became." The 25-year horizon didn't just change his goals; it changed his energy.

When the horizon extends, the architecture changes. VanDuyne didn't just work harder—he architected an entirely new growth model. In 2018, IMEG created an internal mergers and acquisitions (M&A) machine—a system for systematic acquisition and integration:

- 20-person M&A team focused on fully integrating targets
- 2-to-3 year total integration program
- Systems to harmonize operations during the first 6 months
- 94.6% key employee retention post-acquisition

THE EXPONENTIAL RESULTS:

- 56 successful acquisitions since 2015 (100% success rate)
- **Revenue growth:** from $50 million to more than $600 million (12x in 10 years)
- **Geographic expansion:** from regional offices to 102 offices in 34 states
- **Valuation:** from $60 million to $1.2 billion (20x increase)
- Zero layoffs during COVID—even gave raises and bonuses

"We reached $500 million two years early, so now we're targeting $1 billion by 2030," VanDuyne says. "But more importantly, we're creating the template for how engineering firms can grow strategically rather than incrementally."

JONATHAN COTTEN: CONSTRAINTS AS CATALYSTS

Jonathan Cotten faced a paradox that would reshape his entire approach: He knew exactly what he wasn't good at.

"I wasn't operationally gifted. I'm not good with technology. I'm not a good manager," Cotten admits.

Instead of seeing these as weaknesses, he recognized them as a blueprint for improvement. If he couldn't do the work himself, he had to build systems that multiplied beyond him. His constraints became his liberation.

Through discovering the principle that "100x is easier than 2x," Cotten realized something profound: When you try to double, you can work harder. But 100x growth forces complete re-engineering. It forces you to abandon optimization for architecture.

HIS TRANSFORMATION ARCHITECTURE:

- Remove toxic elements that inhibit multiplication
- Establish bulletproof processes anyone can execute
- Deploy talent strategically—find who, not how
- Maintain creative tension between systems and innovation
- Measure everything meaningful

THE EXPONENTIAL RESULTS:

- **2021:** $19 million, handful of stores
- **2024:** $68.6 million, 42 stores
- **Growth:** 260% revenue increase, 53.2% CAGR

"Being responsible for forty-two stores is far easier than having four," Cotten discovered. But Cotten's ambition has evolved beyond adding stores. He's architecting what could become the industry standard—a model where retailers license his systems without traditional franchise constraints.

JEFF BEZOS: THE CASCADE OF IMPOSSIBLE AMBITIONS

While Walker, VanDuyne, and Cotten demonstrate greater ambition at the enterprise level, Jeff Bezos shows what happens when you apply 100x thinking to reshape civilization itself.

In 1994, Bezos quit his job on Wall Street to sell books from his garage. His boss tried to talk him out of it: "This sounds like a good idea, but it would be a better idea for somebody who didn't already have a good job."

Everyone saw an online bookstore. Bezos saw the infrastructure for selling everything—and beyond that, the funding mechanism for his ultimate ambition: getting humanity into space.

This cascading ambition shows how breakthrough entrepreneurs layer their visions:

- **Level 1:** Build a successful online bookstore.
- **Level 2:** Create the Everything Store.
- **Level 3:** Build infrastructure for all Internet commerce (Amazon Web Services, now the world's largest cloud platform).
- **Level 4:** Use wealth to make space accessible (Blue Origin, his private aerospace company).
- **Level 5:** Enable millions to live and work in space.

The progression from books to space:

- **1997 IPO:** \$147.8 million revenue, books only, \$18/share
- **2025:** \$716.9 billion in revenue, approximately 1.58 million employees
- **Market value increase:** exponential (from \$438 million at IPO to \$2.49 trillion by year-end 2025)
- **Space investment through Blue Origin:** more than \$14 billion

"The only way I can see to deploy this much financial resource is by converting my Amazon winnings into space travel," Bezos explained. "Blue Origin is expensive enough to be able to use that fortune."

His "Day One" philosophy maintains start-up intensity at massive scale: "Day Two is stasis, followed by irrelevance, followed by excruciating, painful decline, followed by death. And that is why it is always Day One."

Bezos didn't choose between commerce and space—he architected commerce to fund his space endeavors. He forced evolution at two levels:

- **Commerce:** Every retailer on Earth had to transform.
- **Space:** Humanity now seriously considers becoming multiplanetary.

The lesson: Greater ambition isn't just about building a bigger business—it's about using business as a platform for impossible dreams.

THE PATTERN HIDDEN IN PLAIN SIGHT

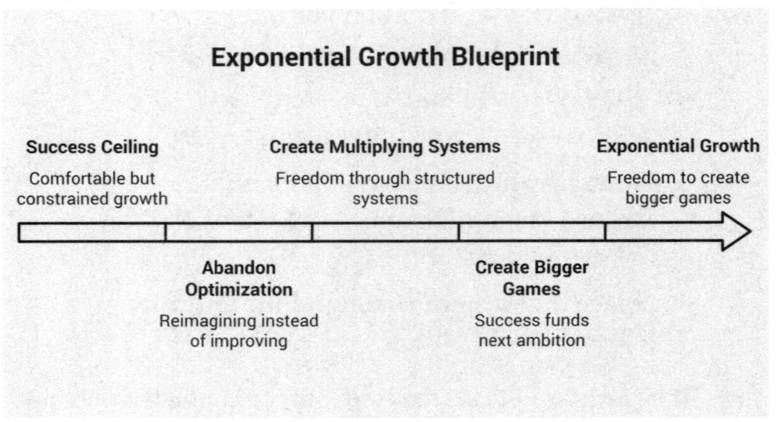

Study every exponential entrepreneur, and you'll find the same pattern. It is the blueprint for exponential growth:

1. **They hit a success ceiling** (comfortable but constrained).
2. **They have a perspective shift** (usually through a question or crisis).
3. **They abandon optimization for architecture** (stop improving, start reimagining).
4. **They create systems that multiply without them** (freedom through structure).
5. **They use that freedom to create bigger games** (each success funds the next ambition).

This isn't a proprietary framework—it's how humans transcend limitations.

BREAKING THROUGH YOUR PSYCHOLOGICAL BARRIERS

Four barriers keep 94.6% of entrepreneurs trapped in optimization. Recognizing them is the first step to dismantling them.

Barrier 1: The Impostor Voice

"Who am I to think this big?"

The Reframe: Walker wasn't special until he joined mastermind groups. VanDuyne was ready to retire. Cotten couldn't manage operations. Bezos was just a Wall Street analyst. Greater ambition isn't about being extraordinary—it's about making the ordinary exponential. It's a decision, not a destiny.

Barrier 2: The Failure Forecast

"What if I aim for 100x and only achieve 10x?"

The Reframe: This misunderstands how ambition works. When you target 100x growth, you architect differently. You build platforms, not products. The architecture required for 100x inherently makes 10x inevitable. Even "failing" by achieving only 10x of a 100x goal puts you in the top 5.4%.

Barrier 3: The Comfort Calculation

"I'm already successful. Why risk it?"

The Reframe: Look at the Fortune 500 from the year 2000—by 2025, 52% no longer exist. They were "comfortably successful" too. In exponentially changing markets, standing still is moving backward. Comfort is the most dangerous risk of all.

Barrier 4: The Resource Restriction

"I don't have the capital/team/time for 100x growth."

The Reframe: Greater ambition doesn't require more resources—it attracts them. Walker's systems attracted talent.

VanDuyne's vision attracted acquisition targets. Cotten's growth attracted the people he needed. Vision precedes resources.

THE FAILURES THAT TEACH

WeWork aimed for a $47 billion valuation—and went bankrupt. Theranos promised to revolutionize blood testing—and collapsed in a fraud scandal.

The difference? They confused ambition with delusion. They prioritized narrative over architecture. Greater ambition isn't about ignoring reality—it's about changing it systematically. Walker tested with two locations before scaling to 14. VanDuyne perfected one acquisition before attempting 56. Bezos dominated books before adding music.

Exponential ambition requires sequential proof.

YOUR AMBITION AUDIT

Before proceeding, assess your current situation. If you answer yes to these questions, you're playing too small:

- Could a competitor buy you tomorrow, and you'd feel relieved?
- Are you solving the same problems you solved five years ago?
- Does your five-year vision feel achievable with current resources?
- Are you indispensable to the daily operations of your business?

If you answered yes to any of these, you don't have a business—you have a costly job.

YOUR FIVE-STAGE ACTIVATION FRAMEWORK

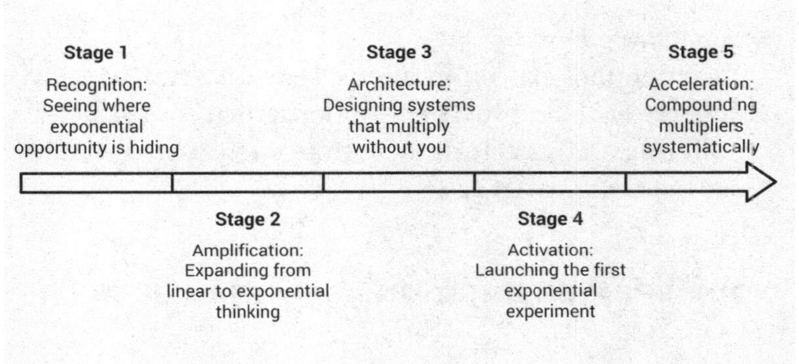

Stage 1: Recognition

Identify where your exponential opportunity is hiding. Document your restlessness. List problems you solve repeatedly. Note what feels "too small." Ask: "What accepted industry constraint would disappear if I thought bigger?"

Stage 2: Amplification

Expand from linear to exponential thinking. What's your current baseline? What would 10x look like? Add another zero—what fundamentally changes? At 100x, how does your entire industry transform?

Stage 3: Architecture

Design systems that multiply without you. Develop operational systems (Walker's checklists). Create growth systems (VanDuyne's M&A machine). Develop platform systems (Cotten's franchise alternative). The test: Can this produce results while you sleep?

Stage 4: Activation

Launch your first exponential experiment. Give yourself 90 days. Design a minimum viable system. Test with a controlled group and iterate based on the data. Success isn't perfection—it's evidence of multiplication.

Stage 5: Acceleration

Compound your multipliers systematically. Quarterly vision reviews. Monthly systems optimization. Weekly metric monitoring. Daily strategic focus time. Each quarter should make the next quarter easier.

YOUR GREATER AMBITION ACTIVATION PLAN

This Week:

- List 10 moments when current success felt too small.
- Identify three problems you solve that thousands face.
- Write one paragraph answering this question: "What would I build with 25 more years?"

Next 30 Days:

- Join a mastermind or peer group of ambitious entrepreneurs.
- Document your 25-year transformation story.
- Share your 100x vision with five people who will hold you accountable.

Next Quarter:

- Choose one process to multiply through systems.

- Create your first operational playbook.
- Remove yourself from one critical function.
- Build a dashboard tracking multiplication, not just growth.

THE CHOICE THAT DEFINES EVERYTHING

Tomorrow, you'll face the same opportunities, challenges, and team. But you now see something invisible to the 94.6%: Every constraint is a multiplication opportunity. Every limitation is a launching pad. Every "impossible" is just "inevitable" waiting to be realized in architecture.

You can close this book and optimize your operations for Monday. Or you can start architecting Monday's revolution.

The market doesn't care which you choose. But in 25 years, you will.

What would the 85-year-old version of you want you to do with Monday?

That's your answer. That's your ambition. That's your beginning.

THE BRIDGE TO GREATER SECURITY

You now have greater ambition. But ambition without protection is delusion. Vision without a fortress is just a vulnerability.

Walker could pursue nationwide expansion because he'd systematized operations. VanDuyne could make bold acquisitions because he'd engineered integration systems. Cotten could grow to 42 stores because he'd built systematic multiplication into his DNA. Bezos could invest billions in space because Amazon's systems operate independently of him.

The 5.4% understand that greater ambition requires greater security—not as protection from failure, but as the platform for fearless execution. Security isn't the brake; it's the launchpad.

Chapter 2 reveals why the most aggressive entrepreneurs are also the most strategically defended—and how to build your Security Stack in 90 days.

Your next 25 years aren't a continuation of the last 25. They're an architectural project. And you've just drawn the first blueprint.

Welcome to greater ambition. Welcome to the Greater Game. Your 100x future is waiting.

ACTIVATE YOUR VISION MULTIPLIER

THE BRIDGE: FROM DREAMING TO ARCHITECTURE

You now understand the paradox that defines the 5.4%: 100x is actually easier than 2x.

When you aim for 2x growth, you optimize your current systems. You work harder, faster, and longer within the existing constraints. It's exhausting because you are fighting the physics of your current model.

When you aim for 100x, optimization is impossible. You are forced to abandon your current model and architect something entirely new. You build platforms, not products. You design ecosystems, not organizations. Like Walker, VanDuyne, and Cotten discovered, this architectural approach requires less effort over time because the systems multiply without requiring additional effort.

Greater ambition isn't about dreaming bigger—it's about architecting differently. It's time to move from inspiration to implementation.

THE MULTIPLIER ACTIVATION: THE 100X ARCHITECTURE DRAFT

This exercise is designed to break the gravitational pull of your current success and prompt you to think in architectural terms. Find a quiet space and dedicate 15 minutes of focused attention to this draft.

Step 1: The Strategic Abandonment

To create a 100x future, you must first dismantle the constraints of your 2x present.

- *Question:* If I were required to achieve 100x of my current impact and revenue within the next 10 years, what operational model, service offering, or core assumption would I *have* to abandon immediately?
- *Example: Roderick Walker had to abandon the idea that he personally managed locations, shifting to an operational platform.*
- *Your answer:* ______________________________

  ____

  ____

Step 2: The Platform Architecture

100x growth requires infrastructure that scales independently of your effort.

- *Question:* What new platform, ecosystem, or automated system would be required to support 100x scale? What is the architecture that makes my effort irrelevant?
- *Example: Paul VanDuyne architected an internal M&A machine, not just acquiring companies one by one.*
- *Your answer:* ______________________________

  ____

  ____

Step 3: The 25-Year Headline

Clarity about the destination accelerates the journey. This is not a goal; it's your inevitable future.

- *Question:* Write the headline of the press release (e.g., appearing in *The Wall Street Journal*, *TechCrunch*, or your industry's leading publication) announcing your achievement 25 years from now.
- *Example: Jeff Bezos, 1994: "Amazon.com Launches the 'Everything Store,' Redefining Global Commerce."*
- *Your headline:* ______________________________

  ____

  ____

The Scorecard: Measure Your Ambition

Now quantify your current level of 100x thinking. Score yourself from 1 (optimization mindset) to 12 (architectural mindset) in each category:

Category	Description	Now (1–12)	12-Month Target
Vision Multiplication	I think in 25-year horizons, not quarterly results.	___	___
System Architecture	I build systems that operate independently and multiply without my involvement.	___	___
Industry Transformation	My goals are not just to grow my company, but to reshape my industry.	___	___
Constraint Liberation	I see every limitation as a multiplication opportunity.	___	___
Strategic Stubbornness	I persist with my vision while staying flexible with tactics.	___	___
Cascading Ambition	Each success funds bigger, more impossible dreams.	___	___
TOTAL SCORE:		___/ 72	

Score Interpretation:

- **6–30:** Trapped in optimization (94.6% thinking)

- **31–50:** Awakening to multiplication possibilities
- **51–72:** Architecting transformation (the 5.4%)

THE DASHBOARD INTEGRATION: ACTIVATE YOUR COMMAND CENTER

Your score is the key to unlocking personalized insights. Don't just read about transformation—systematize it.

Scan the QR code below or go to TheGreaterGameDashboard.com and input your Greater Ambition score.

This action activates your personalized **Entrepreneurial Command Center.** Here's what happens next:

1. **Benchmarking:** The platform will instantly benchmark your ambition level against the top 5.4% of performers identified in our proprietary monthly **Entrepreneurial Pulse** research.
2. **The GMI Impact:** Your Greater Ambition score is the first input into your overall **GMI**—the composite metric tracking your journey to a 100x future.
3. **The Growth Playbook:** The dashboard analyzes your score to begin generating your personalized **Growth Playbook,** identifying

the specific strategies needed to turn your 100x vision into architectural reality.

Your future is bigger than your past—but only if you think bigger than your present. Activate your dashboard now.

CHAPTER 2

GREATER SECURITY—THE FOUNDATION THAT MAKES EVERYTHING POSSIBLE

The most aggressive entrepreneurs are also the most protected. They don't gamble—they architect certainty.

THE PARADOX OF BOLD PROTECTION

You just made a decision.

In Chapter 1, you activated greater ambition—choosing to join the 5.4% who think architecturally about exponential growth. Walker's platform vision. VanDuyne's billion-dollar target. Cotten's industry transformation.

These aren't just inspiring stories. They're your new benchmarks.

Now comes the question that completes your Foundation for Freedom: How do you pursue 100x growth without risking everything you've already created?

Here's what the 94.6% get wrong: They think security and ambition are opposites. They believe you must choose between protecting what you have and reaching for what's possible. They see security as a brake pedal.

The 5.4% know better. They see security as a launchpad.

Greater security isn't about protection—it's about permission. It's about architecting invincibility. It allows your ambition to run free, knowing the foundation is solid. Right now, more entrepreneurs than ever are realizing they don't just need better advice—they need better architecture. They recognize the massive cost of the VFO gap—the chasm between fragmented traditional advice and coordinated virtual family office orchestration.

Structure creates freedom. The more bulletproof your foundation, the more aggressive your expansion.

THE 18-MONTH WINDOW

Remember the convergence we discussed in the Introduction? Here's how it's reshaping the advisory landscape. As you read this, 59.2% of entrepreneurs report they'll likely change their primary financial advisor in the next 24 months—a revolution in advisory relationships is underway.

This is not a trend; it's a revolution driven by complexity. The majority (53.9%) of entrepreneurs consider quality of advice a critical evaluation metric for their financial advisors—it's not just about the numbers anymore. They're switching because their current advisors are trapped in yesterday's game while the entrepreneurs are building tomorrow's transformation. They are seeking architects, not vendors.

The following 18 months will determine whether you're building on sand or stone.

THE SECURITY MULTIPLICATION EFFECT

42.7%

That's how many entrepreneurs worth more than $50 million say their clear sense of security enables them to pursue significant opportunities consistently—not despite being protected but because of it.

They don't build walls. They build springboards.

While the 94.6% agonize over every decision—wondering whether this move destroys everything—the 5.4% have already engineered destruction out of the equation. They sleep soundly while making bolder moves than ever before.

CEG Insights' study of 3,108 entrepreneurs[3] reveals the crisis you're already sensing:

- 84.6% need succession planning—only 21.7% receive it
- 79.2% want nonliquid asset guidance—only 17.2% get it
- 83.5% expect estate planning—only 42% receive adequate help

These aren't service gaps. They're $100 million vulnerabilities disguised as unmet needs. They are the VFO gap realized, and they are costing you millions in overlooked opportunities and unnecessary risk.

The 5.4% don't avoid risk. They **systematically mitigate it** through coordinated architecture. They achieve this through three primary architectures: structural diversification, IP fortification, and organizational resilience.

[3] CEG Insights, "The Entrepreneur and Business Owner Study," 2025. Survey of 3,108 entrepreneurs.

SCOTT AKERLEY: MASTERING STRUCTURAL DIVERSIFICATION

Scott Akerley, former CEO of Pango Group (a Southern California–based escrow and real estate settlement services company), embodies a truth that separates the 5.4% from everyone else: While only 20.7% of typical entrepreneurs feel secure enough to pursue significant opportunities consistently, 58.2% of the 5.4% do. They see security not as protection from failure but as architecture for exponential growth. Akerley mastered this through structural diversification.

THE STARTING POINT: ONE BOLD BET

In 1995, Akerley founded an escrow company with a vision that went beyond traditional service models. Five years in, he made the move that revealed his actual game. He deployed $500,000—over $900,000 in today's dollars—into what seemed unrelated: a joint venture with a luxury real estate brokerage.

Most saw diversification. Akerley saw the first pillar of invincibility.

"We designed the business like a well-balanced portfolio—different markets, different partners, different cycles," Akerley explains. "This wasn't random diversification. This was systematic risk elimination." It was intentional architecture.

THE 25-YEAR ARCHITECTURE

Akerley's formula was precise.

- Form capital-efficient joint ventures.
- Use C corps and LLCs to isolate risk.

- Retain ownership stakes while distributing the burden.
- Add data analytics to spot threats early.
- Repeat until concentration risk is significantly reduced.

"We could tell right away whether conditions were putting us in jeopardy," says Akerley. "Then we'd adjust to sidestep those risks."

While competitors flew blind, Akerley had radar.

THE COMPOUND EFFECT

By 2021, the architecture had scaled.

- 30+ companies and joint ventures
- 300+ employees
- Multiple uncorrelated revenue streams

Akerley tracks what he calls his **Fortress Metrics**—the numbers that prove his business can withstand any storm:

- No client over 5% of revenue
- 90% of customers under 1% each
- Zero partner dependency
- Minimal concentration risk

THE PREMIUM EXIT

When an S&P 500 firm acquired Akerley's $80 million enterprise for nine figures, it wasn't buying cash flow. It was buying certainty. It was buying architecture.

- Initial investment: ~$500,000
- Revenue: $80 million
- Exit valuation: Nine figures
- Return multiple: 160x+
- Time: 26 years of systematic architecture

The acquirer paid a premium not despite but *because of* the 30+ companies. Every additional venture didn't add risk—it divided it. Diversification became multiplication.

From $500,000 to $80 million in revenue to a nine-figure exit. From one company to 30+. From total risk to zero concentration.

That's greater security.

KATRINA LAKE: MASTERING IP FORTIFICATION

Katrina Lake, founder of Stitch Fix, proves that greater security isn't about having massive resources—it's about architecting protection from the start. Security is a mindset, not a balance sheet. She mastered the architecture of IP fortification.

THE STARTING POINT: ONE BOLD REJECTION

2011, San Francisco. Lake had $5,000 in savings and an idea that 100+ investors would reject: personalized styling delivered through data and human curation.

Most saw rejection as failure. Lake saw it as freedom to architect on her own terms.

"I wanted to build it my way," she told *Forbes*, not out of stubbornness but out of strategic vision.

Where Akerley diversified through ventures, Lake fortified through IP and architectural discipline. She built moats where others built inventory.

Lake's formula was precise protection without capital.

Intellectual Property Fortification:

- Patented styling algorithms before competitors noticed
- Created technical moats in the fashion industry
- Built defensible IP worth more than inventory
- Turned data into an impenetrable fortress

Asset Isolation Architecture:

- Kept personal finances completely separate from day one
- Used trust structures before revenue even existed (proactive protection, not reactive defense)
- Protected family wealth from business volatility
- Maintained control through dual-class shares

Risk Distribution Model:

- Subscription revenue (predictable, recurring)
- No retail concentration or inventory risk
- Data-driven purchasing (minimal waste)

"Protect your vision so you can scale without fear," Lake advises.

By 2017:

- Initial investment: $5,000
- IPO valuation: $1.1 billion
- Control retained: majority voting power

By 2025:

- Net worth: ~$380 million
- Freedom achieved: stepped back as CEO in 2021
- Legacy secured: philanthropy and mentoring

THE ARCHITECTURE LESSON

Lake didn't just reject 100+ investors—she rejected their model of growth at any cost. Instead, she built:

- Algorithms that created competitive moats
- Trust structures that protected personal assets
- Subscription models that eliminated inventory risk
- Dual-class shares that preserved control

From $5,000 to $1.1 billion. From 100 rejections to IPO. From bootstrap vulnerability to architected invincibility.

Lake's story destroys the myth that you need millions to build security. What you really need is architecture.

JENNIFER BORISLOW: MASTERING ORGANIZATIONAL RESILIENCE

While Akerley built security through financial diversification and Lake built it through IP fortification, Jennifer Borislow, founding principal and CEO of Borislow Insurance, demonstrates a third critical architecture for invincibility: organizational resilience. Here's what separates the 5.4% from everyone else: 49.1% invest systematically in skill enhancement, mentorship, and leadership growth, while only 22.1% of the 94.6% do the same. They understand this isn't just an operational strategy—it's a foundational security measure that eliminates founder dependency and protects enterprise value from external shocks.

Borislow has secured her particular fortress—a benefits-focused advisory firm serving 300+ employers—multiple times during the past four decades.

Borislow started the business herself in 1982, growing from a one-woman show ("dialing for dollars," as she puts it) to an enterprise with more than 80 employees across 14 states.

A key foundation of that success—and her security—has been people. While the 94.6% view staff as an expense that increases overhead risk, Borislow has always viewed the people she hires and works with as investments that decrease it. "Ever since my first hire back in 1985, I've understood that it's the people around me who give me the security and confidence to aim higher and take things from good to great," she says.

Her investments in people—always ahead of the curve, always strategic—built layers of capability that compounded over time. That fortress of resilience paid off tremendously during the COVID-19 pandemic. While competitors struggled, Borislow Insurance transitioned seamlessly to a remote work environment. "We never missed a beat, because the team was so strong," she says. This is security in action: architecture that withstands external shocks.

The strong foundation of people also gave Borislow the security and confidence to execute a significant strategic transaction—selling the firm in 2019 to Acrisure, a global fintech leader. The organization's strength ensured the transition wouldn't erode value.

Note: The entrepreneurs profiled in this chapter—Akerley, Lake, and Borislow—represent real individuals whose stories illustrate different approaches to building security. However, individual results vary significantly based on circumstances, timing, market conditions, and execution. The strategies described are complex and fact-specific. The contrast is meant to show the difference architecture can make, not to guarantee any particular outcome.

Whether through diversified assets (Akerley), fortified IP (Lake), or organizational resilience (Borislow), the lesson is the same: Security is architected, not accidental. Yet, most entrepreneurs remain dangerously exposed.

THE ENTREPRENEUR SECURITY CRISIS

Dan and John discovered through their own crashes—bankruptcy and family collapse—that success without security is fleeting.

The data confirms the crisis you're sensing:

- The majority (67.1%) face cash flow or liquidity challenges despite running profitable businesses.
- 43.6% recognize they need risk management help—yet most aren't receiving adequate guidance.

This isn't because they don't value protection. It's because most advisors offer products, not architecture. They're playing checkers while you need three-dimensional chess. They offer fragmented compliance when you need an orchestrated strategy.

THE SIX PILLARS OF STRATEGIC SECURITY

Concentration risk is the silent killer of entrepreneurial wealth. The research reveals that:

- 59.2% own 100% of their primary business.
- 70.4% own only one company.
- Entrepreneurs often rely on four or more specialized advisors across personal and business needs—creating fragmentation, misalignment, and coordination chaos.

What percentage of your net worth is in your primary business?

This is the single most dangerous metric in your financial life.

If it's over 50%, you're vulnerable. If it's over 80%, you're one disruption from disaster. This is the primary indicator that you require VFO-level orchestration.

The challenge isn't mastering these domains. It's orchestrating them simultaneously—as the 5.4% do. Miss one, and the others crumble.

1. Investment Architecture

Your business is your greatest asset and your most significant risk. Proper security requires multiple uncorrelated revenue streams.

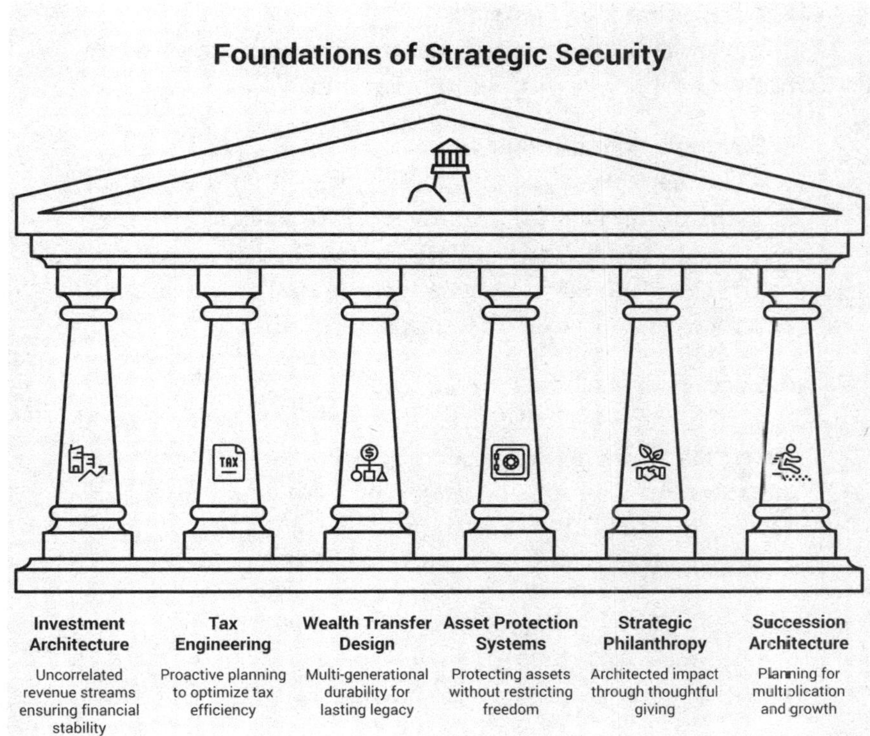

2. Tax Engineering

What is the difference between reactive filing and proactive engineering? Millions at exit. Despite 84.7% expecting tax planning, only 47% report receiving it—that gap costs millions.

3. Wealth Transfer Design

The $124 trillion transfer is happening now.[4] Without architecture, the devastating pattern holds: Most family wealth doesn't survive the third generation.

[4] Cerulli Associates, "U.S. High-Net-Worth and Ultra-High-Net-Worth Markets 2024," estimates $124.3 trillion in wealth transfers through 2048.

4. Asset Protection Systems

Every additional zero in net worth adds a target. Structures must protect without imprisoning.

5. Strategic Philanthropy

The 5.4% don't just give money; they architect impact. Two-thirds (67.3%) run initiatives creating lasting community and industry transformation—nearly triple the rate of others (24.1%). They strategically use giving to reduce taxes, enhance their legacy, and multiply their influence.

6. Succession Architecture

An incorrect structure results in unnecessary taxes and potential chaos. While 84.6% of entrepreneurs expect succession planning support from their advisor, only 21.7% receive it. This isn't planning for death; it's planning for multiplication.

THE FOUR MYTHS DESTROYING YOUR SECURITY

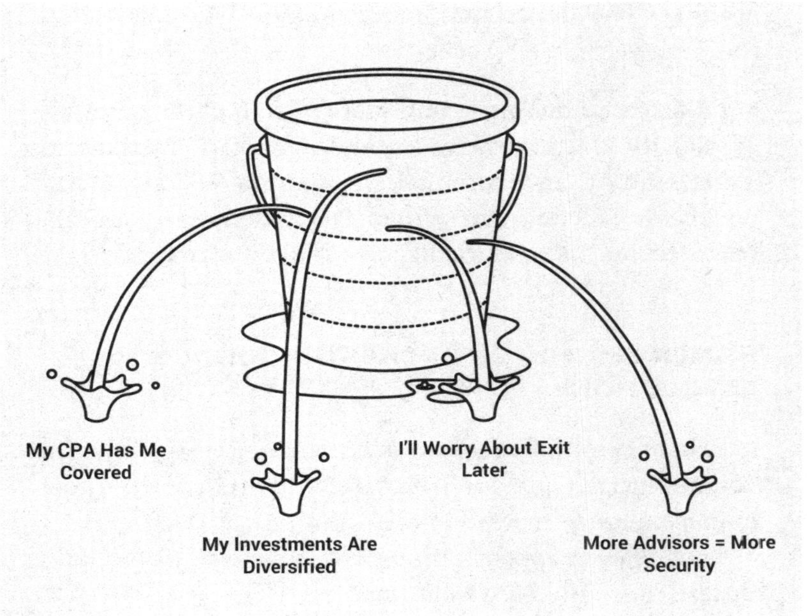

These myths keep the 94.6% vulnerable. The 5.4% dismantle them.

Myth 1: My CPA Has Me Covered.

Reality: CPAs are trained in compliance, not strategy. They report the news; they don't make the news. Only 47% of entrepreneurs receive tax planning, despite 84.7% expecting it. Your CPA is essential, but they are not your architect.

Myth 2: My Investments Are Diversified.

Reality: Owning 50 stocks doesn't matter if 80% of your net worth is in one business. Proper diversification requires uncorrelated assets.

Myth 3: I'll Worry About Exit Later.

Reality: By the time you're ready to exit, it's too late to optimize. The highest multiples go to those who engineered their exit years in advance.

Myth 4: More Advisors Means More Security.

Reality: Uncoordinated experts create gaps. Integration matters more than accumulation. This is the VFO gap. Without a central orchestrator (a financial quarterback), you don't have a team; you have a collection of expensive vendors.

HOMER SMITH: THE ORCHESTRATION REVOLUTION

Homer Smith was the quintessential successful advisor. Top producer at a major firm. $100 million in assets under management. Respected in the community.

But he was trapped in the 94.6% game—selling products instead of architecting solutions.

"I realized I was optimizing a broken system," Smith recalls. "My clients needed orchestration, and I was offering instruments."

THE DISCOVERY THAT SHOULD TERRIFY YOU

Smith shifted his focus to ultra-high-net-worth entrepreneurs (more than $25 million). He started conducting comprehensive audits of their entire financial architecture.

The discovery: Every single ultra-high-net-worth family had significant gaps—gaps created by the very advisors they trusted.

Every. Single. One.

"Doesn't matter who their advisor was," Smith states. "We always found gaps."

This isn't an indictment of their advisors; it's an indictment of the fragmented system within which they operate. Even the best specialists miss the big picture if no one is orchestrating it.

THE 10X TRANSFORMATION

Smith's breakthrough: Instead of pitching investments, he starts with comprehensive security audits (the Second Opinion service).

The diagnostic process is so valuable that entrepreneurs willingly open their financial architecture for review—often uncovering blind spots worth millions before moving a single asset.

THE 100X GAP: THE COST OF FRAGMENTATION

Why are entrepreneurs willing to pay these fees simply for a diagnosis? Because the value unlocked by this orchestration isn't incremental; it's exponential. It reveals the massive arbitrage between the value realized through fragmented, transactional compliance and the potential unlocked through coordinated strategic architecture.

THE 100X GAP: WHEN COORDINATION BECOMES MULTIPLICATION

We witness this transformation repeatedly in CEG's elite VFO programs. Nate Brown, a financial advisor who's mastered the art of VFO coordination, recently shared a case that crystallizes the magnitude of opportunity hiding in plain sight.

THE $26 MILLION WAKE-UP CALL

A successful real estate investor—let's call him the Developer—had achieved everything the American Dream promises: $26 million under management with a major firm, 15 commercial and residential properties, and $1.3 million in adjusted gross income. Yet he was hemorrhaging wealth through the gaps between his advisors.

The twist? The Developer didn't even approach Brown directly. He came through a mutual client, a business empire owner who refuses to meet with wealth managers ever since having a bad experience but raves about his CPA, whom Brown had transformed through VFO collaboration.

"The CPA brought the Developer's case to me for collaborative design," Brown recalls. "In one Wednesday session, after getting the referral Monday, we identified $150,000 in immediate tax savings for 2025—just picking low-hanging fruit off the wealth enhancement strategy tree."

Here's where the story becomes instructive for every entrepreneur reading this.

Before VFO coordination:

- CPA's typical tax return revenue: $2,000
- Value delivered: basic compliance
- Client protection: zero (15 properties in personal name)
- Strategic planning: none

After VFO orchestration:

- Client's captured value: $150,000+ in Year-One tax savings alone

- Additional value: complete asset protection restructuring, estate planning optimization, multi-year tax strategies
- Total wealth impact: millions in protected assets and compound tax savings

That's a **dramatic value multiplication**—the value captured exceeded the typical engagement by orders of magnitude, starting with $150,000 in immediate benefits.

THE MILLION-DOLLAR REVELATION

The Developer's response during that Thursday morning joint meeting should resonate with every entrepreneur who thinks they're well advised:

"I'm not getting any of this from my CPA. I'm not getting any of this from my wealth manager. I'm not getting any of this from anybody."

This isn't about incompetent advisors. The Developer's existing team is sophisticated. His CPA is competent. But as Brown explained: "Even very sophisticated individuals are completely underserved when it comes to the left hand knowing what the right hand is doing."

THE CASCADE EFFECT

The most striking element? Brown hasn't even met the referring business owner, who controls $20 million in assets. Yet this entrepreneur is so impressed by the value his CPA now delivers through VFO coordination that he's become Brown's advocate without ever being his client.

This is the power of orchestration: When you transform how advisors collaborate, the value multiplication is so dramatic that clients become evangelists before they even engage directly.

As Brown observed with characteristic precision, "The reality is most people are being poorly served. I found another one earlier today."

Another one. Another entrepreneur with millions at risk through coordination gaps. Another 100x opportunity waiting to be unlocked.

The difference wasn't better products or more competent advisors. It was systematic orchestration—the transformation that occurs when fragmented expertise becomes coordinated architecture.

WHY 96% SAY YES

"Entrepreneurs are builders," Homer Smith explains. "Once they see their wealth architecture has massive flaws, they can't not fix it."

The math is undeniable: Comprehensive advisory relationships correlate with higher net worth.

The pattern is consistent: Coordinated architecture **correlates strongly** with wealth preservation and growth.

The value multiplication extends beyond traditional planning. One entrepreneur-musician working with a VFO structure saved $4 million in taxes while gaining real-time business oversight and proactive health management—turning vulnerabilities into growth multipliers.

THE VIRTUAL FAMILY OFFICE REVOLUTION

For decades, family offices required more than $150 million to justify costs.

That constraint just evaporated.

The VFO is the architecture that solves this crisis of complexity. It democratizes the expertise previously reserved for billionaires, delivering coordinated orchestration across the Six Pillars.

- **Without VFO:** You're the general contractor coordinating subcontractors who don't talk. You bear the risk of their fragmentation.
- **With VFO:** You have an architect and general contractor handling everything. You shift from being an operator to being the owner of your wealth.

THE SECURITY ARCHITECTURE FRAMEWORK

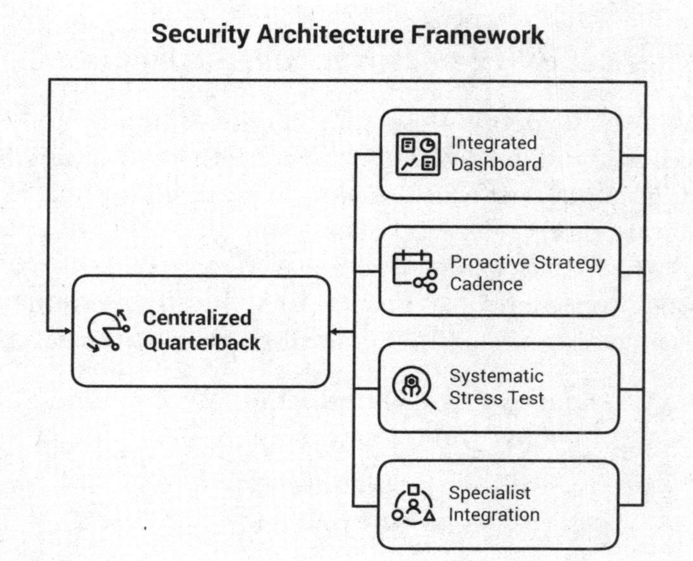

Step 1: The Centralized Quarterback

Identify one person responsible for orchestration. This is your VFO lead—the architect who sees the whole picture.

Step 2: The Integrated Dashboard

Centralize all data. If you can't see it, you can't secure it. (This is what your personalized Greater Game Dashboard provides.)

Step 3: The Proactive Strategy Cadence

Shift from reactive compliance to proactive engineering—quarterly strategy sessions involving all specialists (CPA, attorney, insurance, investments) simultaneously.

Step 4: The Systematic Stress Test

Annual "second opinions" to identify gaps before they become crises.

YOUR SECURITY ARCHITECTURE BLUEPRINT

If you do nothing else from this chapter, start with the Second Opinion Service. As Homer Smith discovered with his ultra-high-net-worth clients: "Every single one had significant gaps. Every. Single. One."

The Second Opinion service begins with a comprehensive diagnostic process that produces what we call a preliminary financial assessment (PFA), a detailed report that reveals:

- Hidden vulnerabilities costing millions in unnecessary taxes
- Coordination gaps between advisors creating dangerous exposure

- Overlooked opportunities worth millions on average (VFO clients' typical discovery)
- Pre-transaction restructuring opportunities about to expire

You wouldn't buy a $50 million company without due diligence. Why run one without it? The essential first step is a comprehensive PFA.

Phase 1: Recognition

Where are you vulnerable? Start with the PFA. Calculate your concentration risk. Identify your coordination gaps.

Phase 2: Architecture

Design your VFO structure. Identify your financial quarterback. Schedule your first Six Pillars coordination meeting.

Phase 3: Implementation

Execute the strategies identified in the PFA. Implement tax engineering. Begin asset protection restructuring.

THE STRATEGIC TRUTH

You've completed Stage 1: Foundation for Freedom.

Greater ambition creates vision. Greater security creates the permission to execute it. Together, they form the unshakable foundation that makes 100x growth possible.

But even the most beautiful foundation becomes a prison without energy. In Chapter 3, you'll discover how the 5.4% build motivation that multiplies—energy that scales, rather than drains, your vision. It's time to build the engine for your empire.

ACTIVATE YOUR STRUCTURE MULTIPLIER

THE BRIDGE: FROM COMPLEXITY TO INVINCIBILITY

You now understand the paradox of the 5.4%: The most aggressive entrepreneurs are the most protected.

The 94.6% confuse complexity with security. They accumulate advisors—a CPA here, an estate attorney there, an investment manager across town—believing more experts mean more protection. But what elite advisors consistently discover is that this fragmented approach creates the VFO gap: dangerous coordination failures, millions in overlooked tax opportunities, and massive architectural vulnerabilities.

The 5.4%, like Akerley and Lake, don't accumulate; they orchestrate. They understand that greater security isn't about defense—it's about permission. It is the systematic elimination of risk that allows you to execute your 100x vision without fear.

It's time to stop hoping you are secure and start architecting certainty.

THE MULTIPLIER ACTIVATION: THE INVINCIBILITY AUDIT

This exercise is designed to expose the two most dangerous—and common—gaps in entrepreneurial wealth: concentration risk and the coordination gap. Be brutally honest; these numbers define your vulnerability.

Step 1: Quantify Your Concentration Risk

Concentration risk is the silent killer of entrepreneurial wealth.

- *Calculation:* (Value of Your Primary Business) ÷ (Your Total Net Worth) = Concentration Risk %

- *Your score: _____%*
- *Reality check: If this number is over 50%, you are highly vulnerable. If it's over 80%, you are one disruption away from disaster. This is the primary indicator that you require VFO-level orchestration.*

Step 2: Identify the Coordination Gap

Fragmented advice is expensive chaos.

- *Question:* When was the last time your CPA, estate attorney, insurance specialist, and investment advisor met *together* (in person or virtually) to proactively coordinate your strategy?
    - [ ] Within the last 90 days
    - [ ] Within the last year
    - [ ] More than a year ago
    - [ ] Never
- *Reality check: If the answer isn't "Within the last 90 days," you do not have a team; you have a collection of uncoordinated vendors. You lack a true financial quarterback.*

Step 3: Name the Single Point of Failure

Identify the single point of failure.

- *Question:* What is the one risk (legal, financial, or structural) that wakes you up at 2:47 A.M.—the vulnerability you know exists but haven't fully addressed? (e.g., "My estate plan hasn't been updated since my last transaction" or "I have no idea if my tax strategy is optimized.")

- *Your answer:* ______________________________

  ____

The Scorecard: Measure Your Security

Now quantify your current level of strategic protection. Score yourself from 1 (exposed) to 12 (bulletproof) in each category:

Category	Description	Now (1–12)	12-Month Target
Concentration Risk	I have wealth beyond business in uncorrelated assets.	___	___
Tax Architecture	I proactively engineer my taxes years in advance.	___	___
Asset Protection	I have strategic separation and asset protection in place.	___	___
Succession Planning	I have clear, tax-efficient transition plans.	___	___
Advisory Coordination	I am in regular communication with an integrated advisory team.	___	___
Systematic Validation	I regularly seek second opinions and stress-test my plans.	___	___
TOTAL SCORE:		___ / 72	

Score Interpretation:

- **6–30:** Vulnerable (high VFO qualification score)
- **31–50:** Protected (coordination gaps likely)
- **51–72:** Invincible (the 5.4% standard)

THE DASHBOARD INTEGRATION: ARCHITECT YOUR INVINCIBILITY

Your scores and the results of your Invincibility Audit are the crucial inputs for diagnosing your structural needs. Don't guess at your security—verify it.

Scan the QR code below or go to TheGreaterGameDashboard.com and input your Greater Security score and concentration risk percentage.

Here's how the platform utilizes this data:

1. Gap Analysis: The dashboard evaluates your concentration risk and coordination gaps to identify precisely where you're vulnerable—whether you need strategic implementation frameworks or orchestrated advisory coordination.

2. Your Recommended Path: Based on your security gaps, concentration risk percentage, and coordination complexity, the platform identifies your highest-leverage path forward:

- **VFO Second Opinion**—If you're losing millions due to fragmented advice, and you require wealth complexity solutions, the Growth Playbook prioritizes this pathway, typically beginning with a comprehensive Second Opinion service. This produces your Preliminary Financial Assessment (PFA)—a detailed review that highlights potential inefficiencies and coordination gaps across your financial structure and clarifies areas that may require further analysis.
- **Strategic Coach Acceleration**—If your primary gaps are execution frameworks and founder dependence, this pathway focuses on operational freedom solutions.

  Review these findings with your trusted financial team to identify coordination gaps, or reach out to us for a VFO Second Opinion.

3. Your Three Moves: The dashboard surfaces your three highest-leverage actions based on your specific security profile.

The 5.4% don't choose between security and ambition. They multiply them together. Activate your dashboard now.

STAGE 2

ENERGY FOR EXPANSION

GREATER MOTIVATION + GREATER PROPERTY

You've built the foundation. Now discover why the most successful entrepreneurs often feel the emptiest—and how to transform that hollowness into your most powerful multiplier.

THE STAGNATION OF SUCCESS

You've done everything right.

Your greater ambition is clear—a 25-year vision that makes today's problems irrelevant. Your greater security is bulletproof—diversified, protected, and architected for invincibility. By every metric that matters to your advisors, your board, and your industry, you've won the optimization game.

So why does success feel like a reckoning?

Why does each new million reveal another mountain you're too depleted to climb?

Why do you have more capacity at $10 million than you're actually using?

Here's the breakthrough the 94.6% never discover: A perfect foundation isn't the destination—it's the platform for your real game to begin. Right now, you're standing on a launchpad, wondering why you're not flying.

THE PARADOX OF PROTECTED EXHAUSTION

This is the cruelest joke success plays on entrepreneurs: The more you optimize, the less you feel. The more you secure, the less you risk.

You've successfully eliminated the external threats that fueled your initial climb—the fear of failure, the adrenaline of survival. But in their absence, you've lost your internal fire.

You've architected invincibility—but invincibility without energy is just sophisticated stagnation.

You've built systems that run without you—but what's the point if you're too depleted to leverage the freedom?

The 5.4% discovered something that changes everything: Energy isn't something you *find*. It's something you *engineer*. And genius isn't something you *have*. It's something you *package*.

WHY EVERY EMPIRE NEEDS AN ENGINE

Think about the entrepreneurs you met in Stage 1:

- **Walker** had vision and security—but needed architectural systems to multiply his impact beyond 70-hour workweeks.
- **VanDuyne** had ambition and protection—but needed a self-generating purpose to sustain a 25-year M&A machine.
- **Lake** had the foundation—but needed to convert her unique expertise into defensible IP before scaling.

They all hit the same wall you're facing: Foundation without fuel is just an expensive plateau.

Stage 2 isn't about working harder—it's about operating from a fundamentally different energy source and capturing that energy systematically. It's the difference between:

- Chasing validation vs. generating purpose
- Consuming energy vs. engineering it
- Hoarding expertise vs. packaging brilliance
- Trading time vs. building assets

THE TWO FORCES THAT CREATE EXPONENTIAL EXPANSION

Greater motivation (Chapter 3) isn't positive thinking—it's the systematic architecture of self-generating energy. It's the discovery that mission multiplied by margin (Mission x Margin) creates a force that attracts A-players, commands premium valuations, and sustains you through decades, not just quarters. Chapter 3 will show you how David Reiling turned banking into a mission that attracted senior executives willing to take pay cuts (the "emotional paycheck"), how Kary Oberbrunner transformed a 70% team exodus into 10x growth, and why internal generation always beats external validation.

Greater property (Chapter 4) isn't just intellectual property—it's the escape from the expertise trap. It's the transformation of your invisible genius into visible, scalable, valuable assets that earn while you sleep. It is the systematic capture of everything you know into frameworks, systems, and methodologies that multiply without you. Chapter 4 reveals how Keegan Caldwell grew his firm 341% by architecting intellectual property into a scalable engine, how

John Kissell's business thrived without him because of his systems, and why every solution you haven't documented is an asset left on the table.

Together, they create something the 94.6% never achieve: energy that multiplies into assets, which in turn multiply into freedom.

THE DEPLETION CYCLE VERSUS THE GENERATION CYCLE

Here's what's actually happening when you can't sleep.

THE 94.6% DEPLETION CYCLE (OPTIMIZATION)

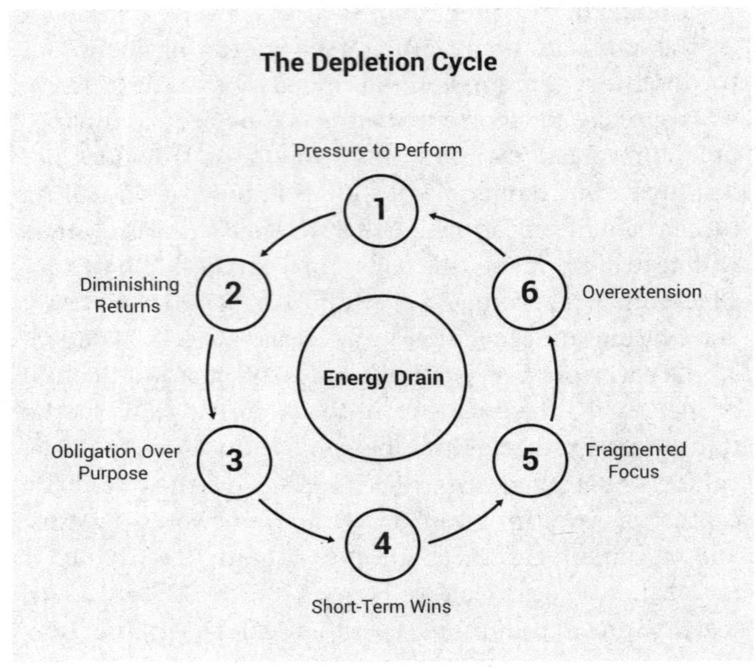

Success requires more effort → more effort creates exhaustion → exhaustion kills creativity → less creativity means working harder → working harder accelerates burnout → burnout destroys value.

You're not tired because you're working too hard. You're exhausted because you're drawing energy from the wrong source.

THE 5.4% GENERATION CYCLE (ARCHITECTURE)

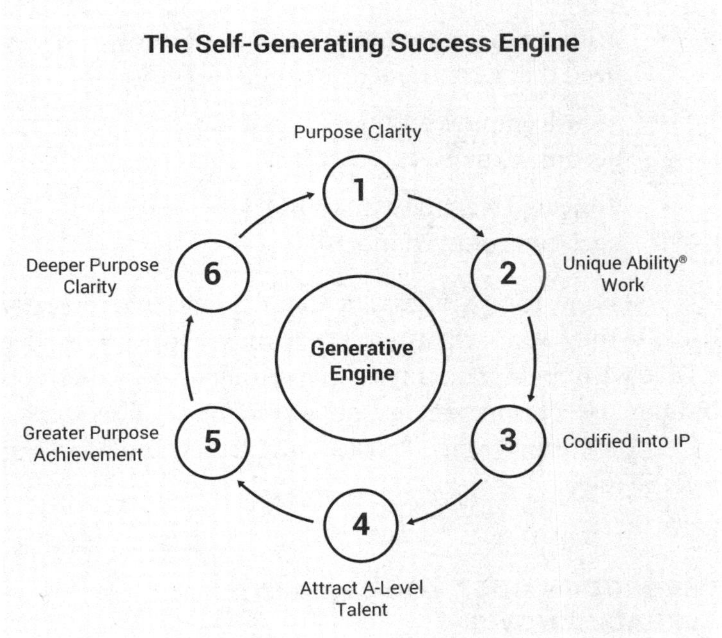

Purpose creates energy → energy fuels innovation → innovation becomes IP → IP multiplies value → value enables purpose → purpose regenerates energy.

You don't need more time off. You need a different engine entirely.

WHAT DIES WHEN YOU SKIP THIS STAGE

We've watched hundreds of entrepreneurs attempt to transition from foundation to scale without first engineering their energy engine. They all hit the same walls:

- Perfect systems run by depleted founders eventually fail.
- Brilliant expertise trapped in one person's head dies with them (the expertise trap).
- Secure empires without energy become expensive museums.
- Protected wealth without purpose becomes golden handcuffs.

You know these stories: The founder who sold too early because they were exhausted. The genius whose knowledge retired with them. The empire that crumbled because it was built on one person's energy, not a systemic architecture.

They skipped Stage 2. They had the foundation but not the fuel.

THE HIDDEN COST YOUR FAMILY ALREADY KNOWS

Your spouse has stopped asking how your day was—they can see the depletion in your posture.

Your kids have learned that successful means absent.

They see what you're just beginning to recognize: Success without regenerative energy isn't success at all. It's just a slow-motion sacrifice of everything that matters.

However, here's what David Reiling discovered: When you shift from external validation to internal energy generation, you don't just transform your business. You transform what you bring home. Instead of being depleted by success, you're energized by it. Instead of your family getting what's left of you, they get the best of you.

WHAT STAGE 2 WILL GIVE YOU

By the time you finish Stage 2, you'll have:

- A systematic approach to generating energy from purpose, not validation
- The blueprint for converting every piece of expertise into scalable IP
- The Mission x Margin formula for attracting A-players
- The framework for packaging your genius into assets worth millions
- Proof that exhaustion is a choice, not a requirement

But more importantly, you'll have something the 94.6% never discover: the energy engine that makes the 100x journey not just possible but inevitable and enjoyable.

THE CHOICE AT THIS PAGE'S EDGE

You can read Chapters 3 and 4 as inspiration—stories of entrepreneurs who found their second wind.

Or you can read them as **engineering**—the blueprint for building an energy system that regenerates rather than depletes, and an IP architecture that multiplies rather than constrains.

The entrepreneurs you're about to meet weren't exceptional. They weren't superhuman.

They just discovered that energy isn't found—it's engineered. That expertise isn't protected—it's packaged and multiplied. That the difference between the exhausted 94.6% and the energized 5.4% isn't effort—it's architecture.

THE MONDAY MORNING QUESTION

This coming Monday, you'll wake up to the same business, the same success, the same security.

But now you face a choice:

Will you continue drawing from a depleting battery, or will you build a generator?

Will you keep your genius locked in the expertise trap, or will you package it into assets?

Will success exhaust you, or will purpose energize you?

Stage 2 isn't the recovery stage. It's the **multiplication stage**—where energy creates assets, assets create freedom, and freedom creates the expansion you've been architecting.

The foundation is built. Now it's time to power the machine that will run on it for the next 25 years.

Turn the page. Your energy—and your empire—await.

CHAPTER 3

GREATER MOTIVATION—ENGINEERING YOUR SELF-GENERATING SUCCESS ENGINE

While others need external charging stations, you generate power from within—then convert that energy into proprietary processes and A-level teams that scale without you.

YOU'VE WON. SO WHY DOES MONDAY MORNING FEEL LIKE A FUNERAL?

You're staring at the projections, wondering why your business is booming . . . but you're not.

The business generates $50 million annually. Your EBITDA multiples would make competitors weep. The board congratulates your quarterly performance. Industry peers seek your advice.

And yet.

You used to love Mondays. Now they feel heavy. It's not because you're failing—it's because you've outgrown what used to excite you. You've discovered the secret that destroys 94.6% of successful entrepreneurs: Every additional zero in your bank account adds another pound to the invisible weight crushing your chest. You've hit the success ceiling, and it's suffocating you.

Let's call it what it is: You're mourning the death of meaning.

The business is thriving. But the part of you that used to leap out of bed with possibility? The entrepreneur who saw problems as puzzles and obstacles as opportunities? That person feels like a stranger. You've become a manager of your success rather than the creator of your future.

Here's what nobody tells you at the IPO party: Success without regenerative energy is just a prettier prison. It's a depletion cycle disguised as achievement.

But what if your energy issue isn't burnout at all? What if it's misalignment—your ambition outgrowing the game you're playing? We've seen it hundreds of times. The very motivators that built your empire—external validation, financial milestones, the thrill of the chase—are now the chains constraining it. You are drawing energy from the wrong source.

Take a moment. When did you last feel genuinely energized by a win? Not relieved it was over, but energized by achieving it?

If you can't remember, you're in the right chapter.

You've architected your 100x vision (Chapter 1). You've built your security foundation (Chapter 2). But here's the brutal truth: Without regenerative energy, your empire becomes your executioner. A fortress without fuel is just sophisticated stagnation.

This isn't burnout. This is something far more insidious: You've optimized yourself into meaninglessness. That may sound harsh, but it's a signal that you're ready for your next jump. It's the sound of your multipliers trying to break free.

Dan Sullivan learned this through bankruptcy at age 35—when every external validator vanished, only internal drive remained. John Bowen discovered it when his family's 400-employee foundry collapsed—external success meant nothing without internal purpose. They rebuilt from zero and learned what the 5.4% know: The entrepreneurs who build quarter-century empires don't *find* motivation. They engineer it. They shift from the depletion cycle to the generation cycle.

THE $100 MILLION ENERGY CRISIS NO ONE ADMITS

Our Greater Multipliers Study worked with 1,016 entrepreneurs. Here is what your advisors won't tell you:

- Three-quarters (74.8%) generate motivation from internal sources—personal pride, compelling vision, or unshakable purpose—rather than external validation.
- Here's the paradox: While the 5.4% are internally driven, they're also 4x more likely to use fear of falling behind as fuel (9.1% versus 2.3%). They don't avoid fear—they weaponize it.
- This dual approach—internal purpose amplified by strategic fear—creates the energy architecture that sustains decades of growth.

But here's what changes everything: The 5.4% who generate internal motivation don't just feel better—they perform exponentially better. They are the ones achieving 100x the results. Their enterprises command significantly higher EBITDA multiples. Their talent acquisition costs drop. Their strategic decisions happen faster. Internal motivation isn't a soft skill; it's a hard asset.

They've discovered the crucial distinction between the two types of motivation and the "paychecks" they generate. It's the shift from chasing a financial paycheck to developing an emotional paycheck.

The neuroscience is undeniable. External motivation (money, status, validation) activates your brain's reward system. This is the hedonic treadmill—each reward requires a bigger hit to feel normal. It is a diminishing returns system (the depletion cycle).

The 94.6% are trying to power a rocket ship with an AA battery.

Internal motivation (purpose, mastery, autonomy) triggers your default mode network—your brain's innovation engine. This system strengthens with use. It is a compounding returns system (the generation cycle).

PRIVATE EQUITY BUYERS CAN SMELL YOUR EXHAUSTION (AND IT'S COSTING YOU MILLIONS)

Here's what your investment banker won't tell you: Private equity (PE) buyers have a term for founders running on external motivation: burned-out sellers. They can smell it in due diligence. They see it in your eyes during management presentations. As a result, they discount valuations by 30–40%.

"When a founder walks in energized by their future, we pay premium multiples," admits a senior partner at a major PE firm. "When they walk in exhausted by their present, we know they'll take any reasonable offer." They aren't buying your past performance; they are buying your future energy. Your energy level is a leading indicator of your enterprise value.

The data is brutal:

- Founders with high energy scores: 12–15x EBITDA multiples
- Founders showing exhaustion: 6–8x EBITDA multiples
- The energy gap: worth up to $50 million or more on a typical exit

Board dynamics shift too. Directors sense founder fatigue and start suggesting strategic alternatives (code for "let's sell before you burn out completely"). Your exhaustion becomes their exit strategy.

But watch what happens when you shift to internal generation: Suddenly, you're playing the long game. PE buyers sense you don't need them. The board sees renewed vision. Your multiple doubles—not because the business changed but because your energy did. Energy precedes economics.

DAVID REILING: THE MULTIPLICATION FORMULA THAT TRANSFORMED BANKING

David Reiling didn't set out to change banking—but that's precisely what happened when he followed what gave him energy instead of what gave him approval. He discovered the formula that solves the energy crisis: Mission x Margin.

"I think making money is easy, to be honest with you. It's really black-and-white. I think it's boring."

These words would sound arrogant if they came from inherited wealth. But Reiling earned his perspective the hard way—proving he could succeed financially in multiple ventures.

Reiling discovered what's destroying you right now: When money becomes predictable, meaning becomes priceless.

THE SECOND PAYCHECK DISCOVERY

The shift occurred while Reiling was volunteering in Tijuana, building homes. He led a team constructing a shelter for a mother with two young children.

"Riding back on the bus that night, I realized I had received two paychecks that weekend," Reiling recalls.

He defined the two paychecks:

- **Paycheck 1: The financial paycheck** (money, status, external validation)
- **Paycheck 2: The emotional paycheck** (meaning, impact, internal generation)

The emotional paycheck was far more valuable because it generated energy rather than depleted it. The 94.6% focus only on paycheck 1, leading to the depletion cycle. The 5.4% architect their lives to maximize paycheck 2, creating the generation cycle.

THE $2.5 BILLION TRANSFORMATION

In his early 30s, Reiling found a failing Minnesota bank—"a train wreck" with $14 million in assets, serving

Hmong and Southeast Asian immigrants that mainstream banks ignored.

"It was the only bank I could remotely afford—and I couldn't even afford that."

He didn't optimize the existing model. He re-architected it around the emotional paycheck.

He focused on serving the underserved—immigrant communities, low-income families, and people that traditional banks ignored. He created products that solved real problems:

- Prepaid cards for the unbanked (which became the industry standard)
- Small business loans for immigrant entrepreneurs
- Financial literacy programs integrated into banking services

THE MISSION X MARGIN MULTIPLIER

Reiling didn't abandon profit for the sake of purpose. He multiplied them together. This is the crucial distinction:

- **The 94.6% operate on an additive model: Mission + Margin.** They attempt to balance purpose and profit, often sacrificing one for the other, which can lead to stagnation.
- **The 5.4% operate on a multiplicative model: Mission x Margin.** They integrate purpose and profit so profoundly that they become indistinguishable from one another. This multiplication is the engine of self-generating energy.

This formula didn't just change lives; it transformed the business.

- **Assets:** From $14 million to $2.5 billion (178x growth)
- **Impact:** certified B corp, Global Alliance for Banking on Values member
- **Innovation:** industry leader in fintech partnerships serving underserved communities

Reiling's organization also became a magnet for A-level talent. Senior executives from major banks took pay cuts to join *the* Sunrise team. Why? Because A-players are starving for meaning, just like you are. They wanted the emotional paycheck. The 5.4% don't compete on compensation; they compete on purpose.

KARY OBERBRUNNER: WHEN COLLAPSE CREATES CLARITY

Greater motivation isn't just about generating energy; it's about resilience. It's about how you respond when the foundation cracks. Kary Oberbrunner faced the ultimate entrepreneurial nightmare: 70% of his team walked out.

Oberbrunner had built a successful publishing and marketing business. His company, Igniting Souls, has published over 2,000 books, many by some of the biggest authors on the planet, which have appeared on countless *Wall Street Journal* and *USA Today* bestseller lists. Revenue grew steadily. Margins were healthy.

But he saw a bigger game: The United States Patent and Trademark Office had an 800,000-patent backlog. Entrepreneurs were losing IP value, waiting years for protection. His vision was a blockchain-based IP solution that was faster, cheaper, and unhackable.

His team's response: mass mutiny.

"Seventy percent of my existing team left—including my COO, CFO, and top salesperson," Oberbrunner explains. "It wasn't very good. I felt alone and abandoned and thought maybe it was time to stop being an entrepreneur entirely."

External motivation would have died here. The board would have called him reckless. Advisors would have preached focus. But Oberbrunner had discovered something more potent than consensus.

THE RESILIENCE ARCHITECTURE

"If entrepreneurs feel they can't put a fence around their ideas, they'll stop creating and innovating," he realized. "By staying focused on that 'why' and the bigger future I could see instead of on the betrayal and fear I felt, I got motivated and creative again. That small blockchain solution became my second company, Instant IP, now scaling across the globe in many industries."

This aligns with research showing entrepreneurs with strong intrinsic motivation demonstrate higher resilience in facing setbacks—they view failure as data, not defeat.

"When adversity strikes, entrepreneurs have one of two choices," Oberbrunner says. "They can fortify their fear or their faith. One leads to stagnation and the other to motivation."

The result: 70% team loss; 10x growth. Zero external validation. Pure internal multiplication.

REED HASTINGS: THE ARCHITECTURE OF PERPETUAL ENERGY

While Reiling focused on Mission x Margin and Oberbrunner on resilience, Reed Hastings, co-founder of Netflix, demonstrates how to institutionalize greater motivation through culture. He built an organization designed for perpetual reinvention.

Netflix has transformed itself multiple times:

- From DVDs by mail to streaming
- From licensing content to creating original content
- From U.S.-only to global domination

Each transformation required massive energy and the willingness to destroy the existing successful model. Hastings understood that the greatest threat to motivation isn't failure; it's arrival.

Netflix's culture (freedom and responsibility; context, not control) is engineered to prevent arrival. They prioritize innovation over efficiency. They hire "stunning colleagues" who are energized by challenge, not stability.

They are perpetually energized by the next transformation, not exhausted by the last success.

ENGINEERING YOUR SELF-GENERATING SUCCESS ENGINE

The 5.4% don't rely on willpower; they rely on architecture. They built a system that manufactures motivation: the flywheel.

1. **Purpose clarity:** Define your Mission x Margin formula. What is the emotional paycheck you deliver?

2. **Unique Ability® work:** Focus your time exclusively on activities that generate the most energy and value.

3. **Codify into IP:** Transform your energized innovation into scalable systems and IP (Chapter 4).

4. **Attract A-level talent:** Use your purpose as a magnet for people who want the emotional paycheck (Chapter 6).

5. **Greater purpose achievement:** Achieve results that reinforce your mission and generate more energy.

6. **Deeper purpose clarity:** Use success to gain deeper insights into your purpose, fueling the next revolution.

This flywheel ensures that every success creates more energy, not less.

YOUR MOTIVATION ARCHITECTURE BLUEPRINT

Phase 1: The Energy Audit (This Week)

Identify your generators (emotional paycheck) and your drains (energy debt). Review your calendar for the past week. What energized you? What drained you?

Phase 2: The Mission x Margin Formula (Next 30 Days)

Define the emotional paycheck your organization delivers to your team and your clients. Articulate your Mission x Margin formula. Share it with your leadership team.

Phase 3: The Flywheel Implementation (Next 90 Days)

Identify one high-drain activity to eliminate or delegate. Block time for Unique Ability work. Begin codifying one energized innovation into IP.

THE BRIDGE TO GREATER PROPERTY

You now have the foundation (Stage 1) and the engine (Stage 2, Part 1). But energy without systematic capture is just expensive enthusiasm. Motivation without monetization is just a hobby.

In Chapter 4, Greater Property, you will learn how to transform this self-generated energy into scalable IP—assets that multiply your impact and your income without multiplying your effort. It's time to turn your genius into your empire.

ACTIVATE YOUR ENERGY MULTIPLIER

THE BRIDGE: FROM DEPLETION TO GENERATION

You've recognized the "Monday morning funeral"—the exhaustion that comes not from failure, but from success without meaning. You are not burned out; you are misaligned.

The 94.6% try to solve this with external fuel: more validation, bigger deals, higher status. They are trapped on the hedonic treadmill, requiring ever-increasing hits of success to feel normal. It is a depletion cycle disguised as achievement.

The 5.4%, like David Reiling, Kary Oberbrunner, and Reed Hastings, discovered a different fuel source: internal generation. They manufacture motivation through the multiplication of Mission x Margin. They don't seek an external paycheck; they generate an internal emotional paycheck.

It's time to stop looking for energy and start engineering it.

THE MULTIPLIER ACTIVATION: THE ENERGY AUDIT

This exercise is designed to expose the misalignment between how you spend your time and what actually generates your energy. It is the first step in engineering your Self-Generating Success Engine.

Step 1: Identify the Generators (the Emotional Paycheck)

Review your calendar for the past week. Look beyond financial success and identify where you felt most alive and engaged.

- *Question:* What three specific activities generated the *most* authentic energy, excitement, and fulfillment? (These are the activities aligned with your Unique Ability and your core mission.)
- *Your generators:*
    - ________________________________
    - ________________________________
    - ________________________________

Step 2: Identify the Drains (the Energy Debt)

Now identify the activities that consumed time but left you feeling depleted, hollow, or frustrated.

- *Question:* What three specific activities drained the *most* energy? (These are often tasks you are competent at but dread, or obligations driven by external validation rather than internal purpose.)
- *Your drains:*
    - ______________________________
    - ______________________________
    - ______________________________

Step 3: The Monday Morning Commitment

The goal is to increase generators and eliminate drains systematically.

- *Action:* Identify one high-drain activity from Step 2 that you commit to eliminating, automating, or delegating starting this Monday.
- *My commitment:* ______________________________

  ____

  ____

  ____

The Scorecard: Measure Your Motivation

Quantify your current energy architecture. Score yourself from 1 (external depletion) to 12 (internal generation) in each category:

Category	Description	Now (1–12)	12-Month Target
Internal Drive	I'm motivated by purpose, not external validation.	___	___
Mission Multiplication	I have a clear formula where purpose x profit = growth.	___	___
Resilience Architecture	I systematically convert setbacks into fuel.	___	___
Creative Destruction	I am energized by reinventing, not protecting.	___	___
Values Attraction	A-players seek me out for meaning, not money.	___	___
Energy Generation	Each success creates capacity for me, not depletion.	___	___
Environmental Design	I have engineered my ecosystem for renewable energy.	___	___
25-Year Energy	My future vision energizes my present action.	___	___
Family Engagement	My success energizes rather than exhausts my relationships.	___	___
Legacy Orientation	I am building systems that outlast me.	___	___
	TOTAL SCORE:	___/ 120	

Score Interpretation:

- **10–40:** External depletion cycle (94.6% trap)
- **41–80:** Transitioning to internal generation
- **81–120:** Self-generating success engine (5.4% zone)

THE DASHBOARD INTEGRATION: ENGINEER YOUR ENERGY

Your Energy Audit and Scorecard provide the data needed to redesign your operating system. Don't let this insight fade—systematize it.

Scan the QR code below or go to TheGreaterGameDashboard.com and input your Greater Motivation score.

Here's how the platform transforms your energy data:

1. **The Motivation Benchmark:** The platform compares your energy profile against the 74.8% of entrepreneurs who generate motivation internally. Track whether you align with the top 5.4% who combine internal purpose with strategic use of external pressures.
2. **The Command Center View:** Your Command Center integrates your Motivation score into your overall GMI (greater multipliers index), tracking how shifts in energy impact your progress across all other multipliers.
3. **Your Recommended Actions:** Based on your energy architecture, the platform surfaces two personalized pathways:

- **VFO Second Opinion**—If your motivation drains stem from wealth complexity and concentration risk, this pathway connects you to solutions that eliminate financial distractions.
- **Strategic Coach Acceleration**—If founder dependence is depleting your energy, this pathway identifies the execution frameworks required to reclaim your time and refocus entirely on your Unique Ability.

The 5.4% don't have more energy—they have better architecture. Activate your dashboard and build your generator now.

CHAPTER 4

GREATER PROPERTY—YOUR GENIUS BECOMES YOUR EMPIRE

While others sell their time by the hour, you're packaging your brilliance into assets that earn while you sleep.

THE $50 MILLION MIDNIGHT CALCULATION

It's late. You're at your desk, calculating something that makes your chest tight.

Revenue: $20 million. EBITDA: $4 million. Industry multiple: 3–5x. Business value: $12–$20 million.

Then you run the nightmare scenario: What happens if you step away for six months?

The answer makes you close the laptop: Your valuation might crater by 70%.

You haven't built a $20 million asset. You've built a $20 million job—the world's most elaborate prison, where you're both the warden and the inmate.

Meanwhile, three e-mails sit in your inbox from competitors who have just sold. One for 8x EBITDA. Another for 12x. The third—a company you considered beneath your notice five years ago—has just been acquired for 15x its value by a strategic buyer.

The difference? They stopped selling time and started selling systems. They transformed their expertise into IP. Their brilliance multiplies in their absence, while yours dies without your presence.

But here's what's really keeping you awake: Your 14-year-old daughter asked you last week, "Dad, what exactly do you do that's so important you miss my games?" And you couldn't give her an answer that made sense. Because "Solving the same problems I've solved for 10 years" doesn't sound important to anyone—especially not to you.

You've discovered your greater motivation (Chapter 3). Energy flows through you again—creative, regenerative, purposeful. However, as David Reiling's banking revolution and Kary Oberbrunner's resilience taught us: Energy without systematic capture is merely expensive enthusiasm.

This chapter completes Stage 2 of the Greater Game Pyramid—Energy for Expansion. You're about to learn how to transform your renewed motivation into intellectual property that compounds. While you sleep, it multiplies without your presence and becomes the cornerstone of your empire—and your legacy.

The good news? Your brilliance is already there. It just needs architecture.

THE EXPERTISE TRAP: WHY YOUR GENIUS IS CURRENTLY TRAPPED

Here's the paradox that traps 94.6% of successful entrepreneurs: The very expertise that built your success is now your most significant liability.

You've spent decades mastering your craft. You solve problems intuitively. You see patterns others miss. You *are* the competitive advantage.

And that's precisely the problem.

If your business depends on your presence, you don't own an asset; you own a job. If your revenue stops when you stop, you haven't built an empire; you've built a dependency trap.

The 94.6% remain trapped here because they believe their expertise is too complex, too nuanced, or too personal to package. They hoard their knowledge, making themselves indispensable—and, therefore, unsellable.

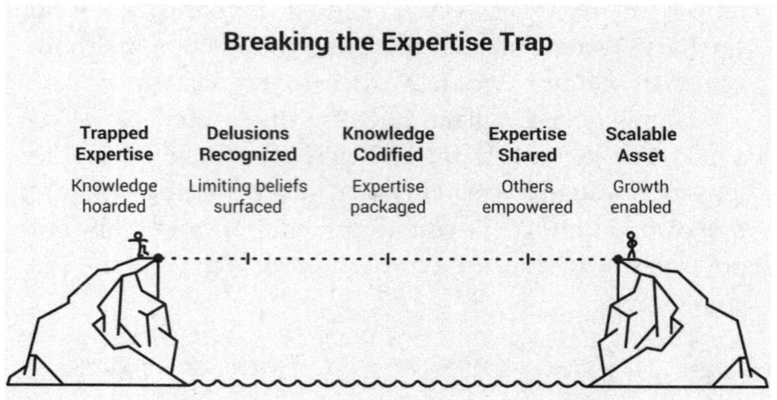

Three delusions trap them:

Delusion 1: My Expertise Is Too Complex to Package.

Reality: Complexity is just clarity waiting to happen. If you can do it, you can document it. If you can document it, you can systematize it. If you can systematize it, you can scale it.

Delusion 2: If I Share My Secrets, I'll Become Obsolete.

Reality: Hoarding knowledge makes you a bottleneck. Packaging knowledge makes you an architect. The 5.4% understand that true power comes not from knowing how to do something but from owning the system that does it.

Delusion 3: I Don't Have Time to Document My Processes.

Reality: You don't have time not to. Every hour spent building IP saves 100 hours of repetitive problem-solving. It is the ultimate time multiplier.

THE VALUATION EVIDENCE: THE COST OF INDISPENSABILITY

The market doesn't reward effort; it rewards architecture. It doesn't value your time; it values your systems.

The "founder dependency discount" is the penalty you pay for being indispensable. Private equity buyers and strategic acquirers systematically undervalue businesses that rely heavily on the founder's personal involvement.

The data is precise:

- **Founder-dependent (the 94.6% trap):** 3–5x EBITDA. Your expertise is trapped in your head.
- **Systematized operations (the transition zone):** 8–12x EBITDA. Your expertise is captured in processes.

- **IP/platform models (the 5.4% zone):** 15–30x EBITDA. Your expertise is packaged into scalable assets that generate revenue independently of you.

On a $4 million EBITDA business, that's the difference between a $16 million exit and an $80 million exit. Your indispensability is costing you $64 million.

The 5.4% systematically transform their invisible genius into visible, scalable intellectual property.

KEEGAN CALDWELL: FROM 80-HOUR WEEKS TO 94% CERTAINTY

Keegan Caldwell was the quintessential successful attorney: Brilliant mind. Winning cases. Working 80-hour weeks. And utterly trapped.

He was trading time for money, constrained by the traditional law firm model. He realized he was solving the same problems repeatedly but capturing none of the systemic value.

"I was a high-paid employee of my own firm," Caldwell recalls.

Caldwell's breakthrough came when he shifted his focus from practicing law to architecting the practice of law. He transformed his expertise into intellectual property.

THE IP ARCHITECTURE:

- **Systematic capture:** Caldwell documented every step of the patent application process, identifying patterns and bottlenecks.

- **Algorithmic optimization:** He developed proprietary algorithms to predict patentability and optimize application strategies.
- **Scalable delivery:** He built a technology platform that reduced a lawyer's work time by almost 50%.

THE EXPONENTIAL RESULTS:

- **Patent approval rate:** from the industry average of 70% to an astounding 94%
- **Revenue growth:** 341% growth in three years

Caldwell didn't just build a better law firm; he built a scalable IP engine. "Intellectual property is the new currency," Caldwell states. "If you're not creating it, you're falling behind."

JOHN KISSELL: THE PLAYBOOK THAT RAN WITHOUT HIM

John Kissell answered a weekend fueling ad in his twenties. The work was too much for one person, so he called friends, paid them out of pocket, and got it done. His boss didn't fire him. He promoted him.

That instinct—solve the problem, systematize the solution, hand it off—became the foundation of a 48-year career in fleet maintenance. Kissell built a $20 million national operation maintaining vehicles for companies like FedEx, UPS, and DHL. High-teen margins after tax.

"Small business, you do everything," Kissell says. "The first year you pay yourself less than everybody else."

What changed was the playbook. Kissell codified every repeatable process into SOPs—standard operating procedures that anyone trained on the system could execute without him.

THE IP ARCHITECTURE:

- **Rapid-deployment SOPs:** A sequenced system for standing up a new fleet repair location anywhere—recruitment, space acquisition, licensing, tooling—each with its own documented process
- **The franchise-without-a-franchise model:** Each technician operates like a franchisee—customer service, parts, repairs, facility management—all within the SOP framework
- **The mentoring protocol:** Structured training that reduced Kissell's involvement on new builds from 50 hours to two

Then, the ultimate stress test. A sudden illness hospitalized Kissell for three weeks,—5% survival odds. What happened to the business?

It ran itself. And it grew.

"The business would actually grow and thrive without me," Kissell says. "It wouldn't just maintain. It would actually increase without me."

Kissell's story is a powerful reminder: Your IP isn't just about scalability; it's about resilience.

SAŠA KRCMAR: THE DATABASE THAT NOBODY WANTED

While Caldwell focused on patentable IP and Kissell on operational systems, Saša Krcmar demonstrates how to multiply IP by recognizing the hidden value that an entire industry dismissed.

In 1999, Krcmar was a land surveyor in Ontario when he acquired a burned-out competitor. Most buyers valued the deal for its client list. Krcmar saw something else: the survey records.

Private survey plans—copyrighted boundary documents—sat in filing cabinets across hundreds of small firms. The profession considered them a nuisance and routinely gave them away for free. Krcmar saw a goldmine. His true asset wasn't the surveying practice. It was the data.

THE IP ARCHITECTURE:

- **The acquisition engine:** He bought 29 companies over two and a half decades—not for their clients, but for their copyrighted records and the research buried inside them.
- **The digital archive:** He digitized more than two million plans onto an interactive map, translating arcane legal descriptions into simple street addresses anyone could search.
- **The public marketplace:** He launched Protect Your Boundaries—a direct-to-consumer platform where homeowners, lawyers, and developers purchase curated survey plans online.

THE EXPONENTIAL RESULTS:

- **Market dominance:** 80–90% of all private survey records in the Greater Toronto Area
- **Multiplication:** copyrighted IP generating revenue around the clock—without Krcmar's direct involvement
- **Strategic leverage:** a brand so powerful that Teranet (Ontario's electronic land registry operator) partnered with him as the consumer-facing retail front end for survey plans

Krcmar didn't just build a surveying practice; he transformed records that professionals gave away for free into a compounding digital asset.

THE COMMON THREAD: THE SHIFT FROM EXPERT TO ARCHITECT

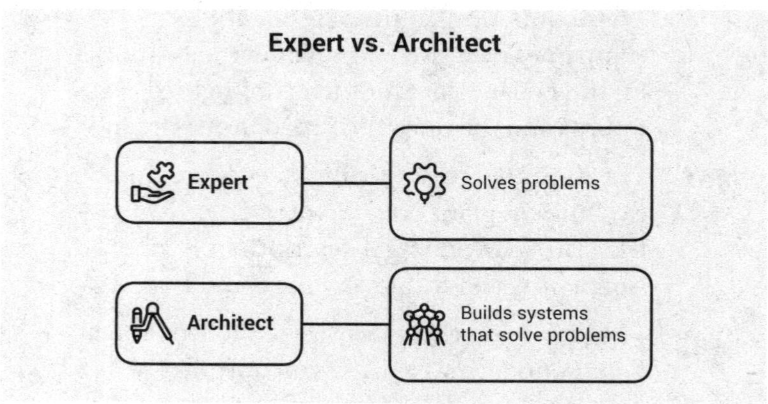

Caldwell, Kissell, and Krcmar didn't have more expertise than you. They architected it differently. They made the crucial shift from expert to architect.

- **Experts** solve problems. **Architects** build systems that solve problems.
- **Experts** trade time for money. **Architects** build assets that generate money.
- **Experts** are indispensable. **Architects** are invincible.

THE IP EXTRACTION BLUEPRINT: HOW TO TRANSFORM YOUR GENIUS INTO ASSETS

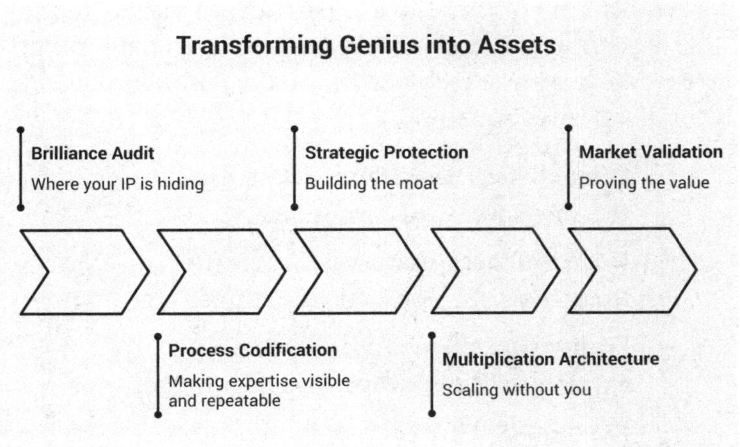

The 5.4% don't wait for inspiration to strike. They systematically extract, package, and monetize their intellectual property. Here is the five-phase blueprint for transforming your genius into your empire.

Phase 1: The Brilliance Audit (Where Is Your IP Hiding?)

Your IP is hiding in plain sight. It's the problems you solve repeatedly, the frameworks you use intuitively, the insights your clients value most.

- **Identify the repeated problems:** What questions do you constantly answer? What challenges do you solve effortlessly?
- **Document the intuitive frameworks:** What are the mental models you use to make decisions?
- **Capture the unique insights:** What do you know that others don't?

Phase 2: Process Codification (Making It Visible and Repeatable)

Transform your invisible expertise into visible, repeatable processes. The goal is to create tools that enable others to execute tasks as effectively as you do, without requiring your direct involvement.

- **Checklists:** These are the sequential steps for successful execution.
- **Decision trees/matrixes:** This is the "if this, then that" logic you use intuitively.
- **Frameworks:** These are visual models explaining the concepts and relationships.
- **Playbooks:** These are comprehensive guides for executing complex processes.

Phase 3: Strategic Protection (Building the Moat)

Protect your IP to ensure it remains a sustainable competitive advantage.

- **Trademarks:** Protect your brand names, logos, and proprietary terms.
- **Copyrights:** Protect your written content, frameworks, and creative works.

- **Patents:** Protect your inventions and unique processes (like Caldwell's algorithms).
- **Trade secrets:** Protect your confidential information and proprietary methods.

Phase 4: Multiplication Architecture (Scaling Without You)

Design the systems that allow your IP to generate revenue independently of your time.

- **Licensing:** Allow others to use your IP in exchange for royalties.
- **Franchising:** Create a replicable business model based on your IP (like Krcmar's Protect Your Boundaries platform).
- **Certification/training:** Train others to deliver your IP through structured programs.
- **Technology platforms:** Embed your IP into software or technology platforms.

Phase 5: Market Validation (Proving the Value)

Test and validate your IP in the market to ensure it delivers measurable results.

- **Minimum viable product (MVP):** Launch a focused version of your IP to gather feedback.
- **Pilot programs:** Test your IP with a select group of clients or users.
- **Iterate and optimize:** Use data and feedback to refine and improve your IP.

THE CHOICE: JOB OR EMPIRE?

You've completed Stage 2: Energy for Expansion. You have the motivation (Chapter 3) and the methodology (Chapter 4) to transform your genius into scalable assets.

The choice is now yours: Will you continue to own a job, trading time for money, constrained by your own capacity? Or will you become an architect, building an empire that multiplies without you?

Will you settle for 3–5x multiples, discounted by your indispensability? Or will you command 15–30x multiples, amplified by your architecture?

The brilliance is already there. The systems are waiting to be built.

THE BRIDGE TO STAGE 3: COLLABORATION AND MULTIPLICATION

You now have the foundation (Stage 1) and the engine (Stage 2). You have a 100x vision, a secure fortress, regenerative energy, and scalable IP.

But even the most potent engine remains constrained without the right environment and the right team.

In Stage 3, you will learn how to multiply your impact through strategic collaboration and empowered teamwork. You will discover how to transform competitors into collaborators (Chapter 5), how to shift from managing people to multiplying genius (Chapter 6), and how to achieve genuine autonomy (Chapter 7).

It's time to move from individual excellence to exponential ecosystems.

ACTIVATE YOUR CREATIVITY MULTIPLIER

THE BRIDGE: FROM EXPERTISE TRAP TO EXPONENTIAL ASSET

You've recognized the $50 million midnight calculation: the realization that you haven't built an asset; you've built the world's most elaborate job.

The 94.6% remain trapped here because they believe their expertise is too complex, too nuanced, or too personal to package. They hoard their knowledge, making themselves indispensable—and, therefore, unsellable. They are trading time for money, ensuring their valuation remains stuck at 3–5x EBITDA.

The 5.4%, like Caldwell, Kissell, and Krcmar, understand that complexity is just clarity waiting to happen. They systematically transform their invisible genius into visible, scalable intellectual property. They don't sell their time; they sell their systems. This is the shift that unlocks the 15–30x valuation multiples and creates true freedom.

Energy without systematic capture is just expensive enthusiasm. It's time to transform your brilliance into your empire.

THE MULTIPLIER ACTIVATION: THE 20-MINUTE IP CAPTURE

This exercise is designed to demonstrate that your expertise can be effectively packaged and that you have the time to do so. You will create your first piece of scalable IP right now.

Step 1: Identify the Repeated Problem (the Raw Material)

Think back over the past month. Identify one significant problem you solved for a client, for a team member, or in your operations that you have solved before.

- *The problem I solved (again):* ____________________
- *Example: how to qualify a high-value lead; how to onboard a new technician; how to analyze a specific type of investment opportunity.*

Step 2: Codify the Solution (the Systematization)

Take 15 minutes to document the solution. Do not write a manual; create a tool. The goal is that someone else could execute this 80% as well as you, without needing to ask you any questions.

- *Choose your tool format:*
    - [ ] **Checklist:** The sequential steps required for successful execution.
    - [ ] **Decision tree/matrix:** The "if this, then that" logic you use intuitively.
    - [ ] **Framework:** A visual model explaining the concepts and relationships.
- *Use a separate sheet of paper or a digital document to create the tool.*

Step 3: Package the IP (the Asset Creation)

Give your new tool a proprietary, memorable name. This is the first step toward trademarking and monetization.

- *My new IP name:*

  ____

- *Example: Caldwell's "Evidence of Use Analysis," Kissell's "Site Acquisition Playbook"*

You have just converted 15 minutes into a lasting asset.

The Scorecard: Measure Your Property

Quantify your current IP architecture. Score yourself from 1 (expertise trapped) to 12 (empire runs without you) in each category:

Category	Description	Now (1–12)	12-Month Target
Documentation Discipline	I systematically capture and document my methodologies.	___	___
IP Protection Strategy	My intellectual property is strategically protected (trademarked, copyrighted).	___	___
Scalable Packaging	My expertise generates revenue even when I'm not involved.	___	___
Licensing Architecture	Others can implement my IP through certification or licensing.	___	___
Portfolio Development	I continually develop new IP assets that compound in value.	___	___
Legacy Readiness	My IP will generate value for generations to come.	___	___
TOTAL SCORE:		___ / 72	

Score Interpretation:

- **6–30:** Your expertise is trapped (2–4x multiple potential)
- **31–50:** You are beginning transformation (5–8x multiple potential)
- **51–72:** Your empire runs without you (10–15x+ multiple potential)

THE DASHBOARD INTEGRATION: TURN GENIUS INTO ASSETS

Your 20-Minute IP Capture exercise and Scorecard are the starting point for quantifying the value trapped in your head.

Scan the QR code below or go to TheGreaterGame Dashboard.com and input your Greater Property score.

Here's how the platform operationalizes this data:

1. **The Founder Dependency Signal:** Your greater property score reveals how much of your enterprise value depends on you personally. The platform calculates your current valuation range and shows what's possible when your IP operates independently.

2. **The Command Center View:** Your property score integrates into your overall GMI, tracking the direct correlation between systematized IP and your multiplication potential across all other multipliers.
3. **Your Recommended Actions:** Based on your IP architecture, the platform surfaces personalized pathways:
   - **VFO Second Opinion**—If your IP is valuable but unprotected or unconverted into wealth, this pathway helps you structure ownership, licensing, and succession to maximize long-term value.
   - **Strategic Coach Acceleration**—If your IP is trapped in your head and limiting your valuation multiple, this pathway provides the frameworks to document, systematize, and scale your methodologies.

If you died tomorrow, would your expertise die with you—or would it continue generating wealth and wisdom for decades? Activate your dashboard and start building your legacy now.

STAGE 3

COLLABORATION AND MULTIPLICATION

GREATER COMMUNITY + GREATER TEAMWORK + GREATER AUTONOMY

You've engineered the energy. You've built the assets. Now discover the paradox that traps the 94.6%: The entrepreneurs who scale fastest are the ones who stop trying to do it alone—and stop trying to be the hero.

THE BOTTLENECK OF SUCCESS

You face a different calculation now.

You're not worried about energy—your greater motivation (Chapter 3) is self-generating. You're not concerned about assets—your greater property (Chapter 4) is documented, protected, and multiplying. By every measure you set for yourself in Stages 1 and 2, you've succeeded.

So why does scaling feel like drowning in complexity?

Why does every new level of success require exponentially more management effort from *you*?

Why are you working harder at $50 million than you did at $5 million?

Here's the revelation that defines Stage 3: You've been trying to solve a multiplication problem with addition tools. You've been scaling through personal effort. You've built an organization where every critical decision, every significant opportunity, and every crisis flows back to you.

You are the bottleneck. And it's killing your growth.

THE INDISPENSABILITY TRAP

You've done everything right—for Stage 2. Your energy is regenerative, your expertise is packaged into valuable IP, and your foundation is bulletproof.

However, what the 5.4% discovered is that a perfect Stage 2 foundation still hits a growth ceiling if the founder remains trapped by the illusion of indispensability. The 94.6% confuse being the hero who saves the day with being the architect who makes heroes unnecessary.

You have a Ferrari engine, but your organizational architecture can't handle the power.

The 5.4% realize that exponential multiplication doesn't happen *through* you. It happens *beyond* you—but only when you architect the sequence correctly.

THE ARCHITECTURE OF EXPONENTIAL SCALE (AND WHY THE SEQUENCE MATTERS)

The 94.6% try to fix their teams first, believing better management will unlock growth. Or they seek autonomy first, attempting to escape the complexity they created. They fail because they violate the sequence of multiplication.

The 5.4% follow a precise architectural sequence: external multiplication → internal excellence → personal freedom.

First: greater community (Chapter 5). You must transform external competition into collaboration BEFORE optimizing internal teams. Why? External multiplication creates the demand that forces internal evolution. This is the shift from zero-sum competition to positive-sum creation through **free zone collaborations.** Chapter 5 shows how Dale Wills transformed his biggest threat (banks) into his greatest multiplier, achieving 10x growth during a recession, how Marc Benioff built a multi-hundred-billion-dollar ecosystem by turning competitors into contributors.

Second: greater teamwork (Chapter 6). Only after unlocking external opportunities can you build the self-managing teams required to execute them. This is the shift from managing people to multiplying genius—creating a culture that eliminates founder dependency (the **indispensability discount**). Chapter 6 reveals how Mike Wandler reduced his workforce from 600 to 250 while doubling revenue and how Kent Pilcher architected teams that allowed him 100+ days off annually.

Third: greater autonomy (Chapter 7). True freedom—invincibility—comes last because it requires both external ecosystems AND internal excellence. This is the ultimate liberation, where your presence becomes optional while your impact becomes exponential (the **absence multiplier**). Chapter 7 demonstrates how Evan Ryan traveled 300 days while his company grew 3x, proving that the business can grow faster without the founder present.

Get the sequence wrong, and you get expensive chaos. Get it right, and you achieve liberation.

THE HIDDEN COST OF HEROIC LEADERSHIP

The market brutally penalizes founder dependency. The "indispensability discount" is the price you pay for being the heroic leader.

- **Heroic leadership (94.6% trap):** You get 3–5x EBITDA valuation multiples. Effort increases with scale. Innovation is founder-dependent.
- **Multiplication architecture (5.4% zone):** You get 10–15x+ EBITDA valuation multiples. Effort decreases with scale. Innovation comes from the ecosystem.

On a $5 million EBITDA business, the indispensability trap costs you $40–$50 million or more at exit.

But the real cost isn't just financial. Your family already knows it. They watch you answer e-mails during dinner "because no one else can handle this." They've learned that "successful" means "absent and exhausted."

What if the very indispensability that makes you feel important is precisely what's keeping your impact small?

THE SHIFT FROM PRODUCER TO PLATFORM

Stage 3 isn't about better management. It's about a fundamental identity transformation from producer to platform.

- **Producers** create value. → **Platforms** multiply value creators.
- **Producers** compete for resources. → **Platforms** architect ecosystems.
- **Producers** are irreplaceable. → **Platforms** are inevitable.

This isn't delegation. It's architecture—designing systems where multiplication is the default, not the exception.

The real revelation? Among the 5.4% achieving exponential growth, 47.2% have fully stepped back from day-to-day operations. They didn't become better managers—they architected systems that eliminated the need for their management.

By the time you finish Chapter 7, you'll have:

- **The ecosystem blueprint:** how to transform your biggest competitor into your greatest multiplier using free-zone collaborations
- **The multiplication system:** how to convert dependent employees into multiplying leaders and eliminate the indispensability discount
- **The invincibility framework:** how to make your presence optional while growth accelerates using the absence multiplier

But more importantly, you'll understand *why* the 94.6% who attempt this out of sequence fail—while the 5.4% who follow this architecture achieve exponential freedom.

THE CHOICE AT THIS THRESHOLD

You can read Chapters 5, 6, and 7 as interesting case studies—stories of entrepreneurs who figured out how to scale by learning from others.

Or you can read them as your **liberation sequence**—the exact architectural order for transforming from the indispensable bottleneck to the invincible architect.

Dale Wills made one phone call on a Tuesday afternoon to his biggest adversary. That's all it took to begin his transformation from fighter to multiplier.

THE QUESTION THAT CHANGES EVERYTHING

This Monday morning, you'll walk into your business with the same energy, the same IP, the same potential you have today.

But now you face a choice that compounds forever:

Will you continue being the indispensable hero who saves the day, or will you become the invincible architect who makes heroes unnecessary?

The engine is built. The fuel is flowing. Now it's time to create the vehicle that runs—and multiplies—without you.

Turn the page. Your multiplication awaits.

CHAPTER 5

GREATER COMMUNITY—YOUR COMPETITION BECOMES YOUR MULTIPLIER

While others fight over market share, you're architecting ecosystems where everyone's success amplifies your own.

THE ALLIANCE NOBODY EXPECTED

You're calculating the compounding cost of competition.

Every strategic planning session ends the same way: defending market share, protecting margins, and outmaneuvering competitors that seem to multiply while you're still adding. The math is working against you. Each year requires more effort for the same results. More battles to fight. More territory to defend.

Your board wants aggressive growth. Your team is exhausted from constant combat. The competitor you've been battling for five years just raised $10 million to "disrupt" what you pioneered.

Here's what's keeping you awake: You've packaged your expertise into valuable IP (Chapter 4), but you're still playing a zero-sum game where every win requires someone else's loss.

The exhaustion isn't just professional—it's personal. Your spouse has stopped asking about your day because the answer is always about battles, not breakthroughs. Your closest friends—the ones who knew you before the success—barely recognize the warrior you've become.

Isn't it fascinating how the harder you fight, the heavier success feels?

The 5.4% who achieve exponential growth have discovered something your advisors won't tell you: Your real competition isn't who you think it is. Your real competition is the belief that business *must* be a zero-sum game.

You didn't misplay the game—you outgrew the field. It's time to build a new stadium.

What if the exhaustion you feel isn't from poor execution but from perfect execution of an outdated strategy?

THE 5.4% INSIGHT: ECOSYSTEMS OVER EMPIRES

Our Greater Multipliers Study reveals the multiplication difference:

- The 5.4% architect collaboration: 78.2% lead high-level communities that create exclusive opportunities and strategic alliances.

- The 94.6% optimize networks: While 37.7% maximize their connections for referrals and collaboration, they remain participants rather than architects.

The distinction is profound: The 5.4% don't join ecosystems—they build them. They transform networking from extraction to creation.

The data is clear: Multiplication requires collaboration. Isolation leads to stagnation.

Greater community isn't about networking or making friends. It's about architecting ecosystems where collaboration is the primary multiplier. It's the shift from competing for market share to creating the market itself.

DALE WILLS: THE $36 MILLION ARBITRAGE

Dale Wills had every reason to hate banks.

It was 2011. The financial crisis had decimated Minnesota's real estate market. Banks were foreclosing on properties, calling in loans, and driving developers out of business across the state. Every strategic consultant said the same thing: Keep your distance. Minimize exposure. Survive.

Dale did the opposite. He saw opportunity where others saw apocalypse.

"The banks were sitting on massive portfolios of distressed assets," recalls Wills. "They didn't want to be landlords. They wanted liquidity."

Wills had development expertise but limited capital. The banks had capital and assets but no development expertise.

He recognized the complementary capabilities—the foundation of what we call a free-zone collaboration.

THE FREE-ZONE COLLABORATION: 1+1=11

A free-zone collaboration is a partnership where both parties bring unique capabilities to create value neither could achieve alone. It transforms adversaries into amplifiers.

Wills approached the banks not as enemies but as partners in solving a mutual problem.

THE ARCHITECTURE:

- **The pitch:** "You have the assets. I have the expertise. Let's develop these properties together and share the upside."
- **The structure:** Wills provided the development services; the banks provided the financing and the properties.
- **The result:** The banks got performing assets and liquidity; Wills got access to prime properties and exponential growth.

THE EXPONENTIAL IMPACT:

- **Growth:** from $4 million to $40 million in revenue in two years (10x growth)
- **Scale:** from small projects to significant developments
- **Leverage:** multiplied his impact without multiplying his capital risk

Wills didn't just survive the crisis; he thrived in it. He transformed his biggest threat into his greatest multiplier.

JOE POLISH: THE POWER OF CURATED CONNECTION

Dale Wills's transformation demonstrates the power of converting adversaries into amplifiers. But greater community extends beyond tactical alliances; it involves architecting entire ecosystems where connection itself is the primary multiplier.

"I had a tough childhood and was starving for connection growing up," says Joe Polish. "I was lonely, and so I don't want other people to be alone."

This drive led him to create Genius Network, one of the world's premier groups for bringing high-level entrepreneurs together.

Genius Network boasts more than 200 members who pay between $35,000 and $100,000 annually. Polish, meanwhile, has an equity stake in 35 companies that were born from his connections. "My philosophy is: I don't just try to increase my slice of the pie; I try to increase the pie," he says.

The architecture of this success is intentional curation. Polish is highly selective about who gets invited—homing in on genuine collaborators eager to share wisdom rather than take from others. He vets potential members by focusing on their values and character—specifically looking for people who are ELF (easy, lucrative, and fun) and avoiding those who are HALF (hard, annoying, lame, and frustrating).

"The quality of the person you're doing business with is as important as the quality of the business that you're doing," he says. "I always want to see how people that are more powerful treat people that are less powerful than them."

The result is that Genius Network members do much more than just network. They engage in deep connecting and relationship building that enables them to accomplish goals they likely couldn't achieve on their own.

"Genius Network is an ecosystem that allows us to do together what we could never do alone," explains Polish.

MARC BENIOFF: THE PLATFORM REVOLUTION

While Wills focused on tactical alliances and Polish on curated ecosystems, Marc Benioff demonstrates the ultimate expression of greater community: building a platform where competitors become contributors.

In 1999, Benioff left Oracle—the epitome of zero-sum, adversarial business culture—to found Salesforce. He had a vision for a new model: software delivered through the cloud.

But the true genius wasn't the technology; it was the ecosystem.

The Oracle Model (Zero Sum):

- Lock customers into proprietary systems.
- Crush competitors through aggressive sales tactics.
- Maximize control and minimize collaboration.

The Salesforce Model (Positive Sum):

- Build an open platform that invites collaboration.
- Empower partners to build businesses on the platform.
- Maximize value creation for the entire ecosystem.

THE APPEXCHANGE: THE BILLION-DOLLAR MULTIPLIER

In 2005, Benioff unveiled the AppExchange—a marketplace where other companies, including competitors, could build and sell applications that integrated with Salesforce. It officially launched in January 2006. This was revolutionary. It transformed Salesforce from a product company into a platform company. It turned competitors into contributors.

The Exponential Impact:

- **Ecosystem scale:** There are nearly 6,000 apps and more than 14 million installs on the AppExchange
- **Valuation:** It moved from its landmark $1.1 billion IPO in 2004 to a peak market cap of more than $327 billion
- **The multiplier effect:** For every $1 Salesforce earns, the ecosystem generates $5.60 — projected to reach $6.93 for every Salesforce dollar by 2028

Benioff didn't just build a company; he built an economy. He understood that the greatest value comes not from owning everything, but from enabling everyone to achieve their potential. As Benioff has long championed, the most powerful business model isn't built on competition—it's built on collaboration.

THE ZERO-SUM DELUSION VERSUS THE POSITIVE-SUM REALITY

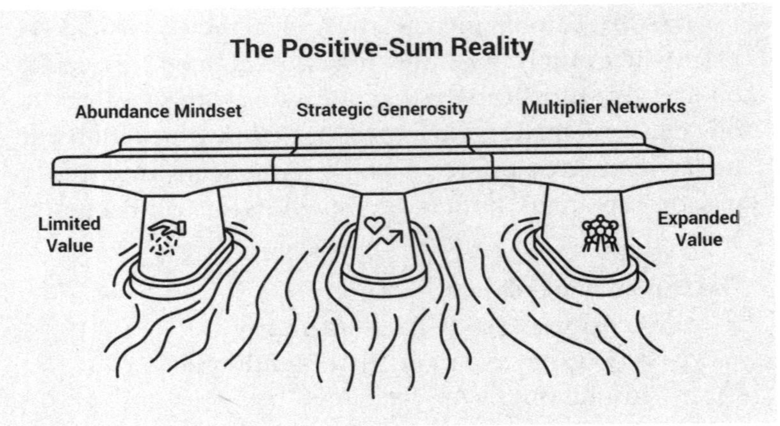

The 94.6% remain trapped in the zero-sum delusion, constrained by three limiting beliefs:

Delusion 1: The Scarcity Mindset ("If they win, I lose.")

Reality: The market isn't a fixed pie. It's an expanding universe of opportunity. Collaboration creates new markets, new value, and new possibilities. The 5.4% operate from an abundance architecture.

Delusion 2: Protectionism ("I must guard my secrets.")

Reality: Hoarding knowledge creates bottlenecks and limits growth. Sharing knowledge strategically builds ecosystems and establishes industry standards. The 5.4% practice strategic generosity.

Delusion 3: Isolation ("I must do it alone.")

Reality: Individual effort is linear; collaborative effort is exponential. The most significant breakthroughs come from the intersection of diverse perspectives and capabilities—the 5.4% architect multiplier networks.

STRATEGIC GENEROSITY: THE ULTIMATE COMPETITIVE ADVANTAGE

The 5.4% understand a powerful paradox: The more you give away, the more you gain.

Strategic generosity isn't about altruism; it's about architecture. It's about sharing frameworks, insights, and opportunities to strengthen the ecosystem and position yourself at its center.

- **Building industry standards:** When you share your frameworks, they become the industry standard (example: Google open-sourcing Android).
- **Attracting A-level talent:** Purpose-driven collaboration attracts top talent who want to be part of something bigger.
- **Creating exponential opportunities:** Generosity creates reciprocity, opening doors to unexpected partnerships and breakthroughs.

When you build the ecosystem, you become the inevitable beneficiary of its growth.

THE COLLABORATION SPECTRUM: WHERE ARE YOU PLAYING?

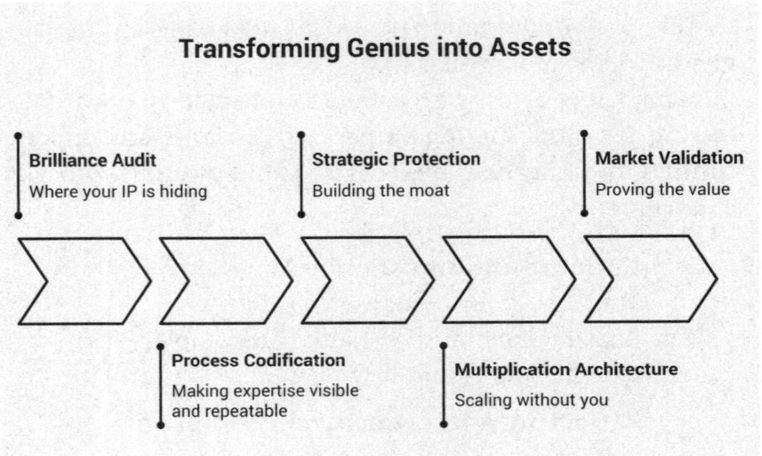

Collaboration exists on a spectrum—the 5.4% play at the exponential end.

Level 1: Transactional (the 94.6% Trap)

Focus on immediate gain. Adversarial relationships. Zero-sum thinking. (Example: Traditional vendor negotiations.)

Level 2: Tactical (the Optimization Zone)

Focus on short-term projects. Cooperative relationships. Limited scope. (Example: Joint marketing campaigns.)

Level 3: Strategic (the Transition Zone)

Focus on long-term goals. Collaborative relationships. Shared risk and reward. (Example: Dale Wills's joint ventures.)

Level 4: Exponential (the 5.4% Zone)

Focus on ecosystem creation. Transformational relationships. Positive-sum thinking. (Examples: Joe Polish's Genius Network, Marc Benioff's AppExchange.)

THE ECOSYSTEM ARCHITECTURE BLUEPRINT: HOW TO BUILD YOUR MULTIPLIER NETWORK

The 5.4% don't network; they architect ecosystems. Here is the four-phase blueprint for building your multiplier network.

Phase 1: Identify the Void (Where Is the Opportunity?)

Identify the gaps in your industry where collaboration could create exponential value. What problems are too big for any single player to solve?

Phase 2: Define the Free Zone (Who Are Your Multipliers?)

Identify potential collaborators—including competitors—who possess complementary capabilities. Where do your strengths align with their weaknesses, and vice versa?

Phase 3: Architect the Platform (How Will You Collaborate?)

Design the structure for collaboration. Will it be a joint venture, a curated network, an open platform, or an industry alliance? Define the rules of engagement and the mechanisms for shared value creation.

Phase 4: Activate the Multipliers (Making the First Move)

Initiate the collaboration. Propose the free zone opportunity. Start with a pilot project to build trust and demonstrate value.

THE CHOICE: COMPETITION OR CREATION?

You have completed the first step of Stage 3: Collaboration and Multiplication. You understand the exponential power of shifting from zero-sum competition to positive-sum creation.

The choice is now yours: Will you continue to fight for market share, exhausted by constant combat? Or will you architect ecosystems where everyone's success amplifies your own?

Will you remain isolated, constrained by your own capabilities? Or will you leverage the collective genius of your community?

THE BRIDGE TO GREATER TEAMWORK

You have learned how to multiply your impact through external collaboration. But actual multiplication requires applying these same principles internally.

In Chapter 6, Greater Teamwork, you will discover how to transform your organization from a collection of individuals into a cohesive, self-managing ecosystem. You will learn how to shift from managing people to multiplying genius, creating a culture where empowerment replaces delegation and autonomy drives innovation.

It's time to move from external ecosystems to internal multiplication.

ACTIVATE YOUR COLLABORATION MULTIPLIER

THE BRIDGE: FROM ZERO-SUM TO EXPONENTIAL ECOSYSTEMS

You've recognized the compounding cost of competition. The exhaustion you feel isn't from working too hard; it's from playing the wrong game—a zero-sum battle where every win requires someone else's loss.

The 94.6% remain trapped in this warfare, fighting for market share, guarding secrets, and optimizing their way to irrelevance.

The 5.4%, like Dale Wills and Marc Benioff, discovered the multiplication paradox: Your real competition isn't your competitor; it's the belief that you must compete at all. They transformed adversaries into amplifiers. They didn't split the pie; they built a bigger bakery. They understand that strategic generosity—sharing frameworks to create industry standards—is the ultimate competitive advantage.

It's time to stop fighting for market share and start architecting the ecosystem.

THE MULTIPLIER ACTIVATION: THE COMPETITOR-TO-COLLABORATOR SHIFT

This exercise is designed to identify your first free zone collaboration—a partnership that creates value neither party could achieve alone. This is the blueprint for transforming your biggest threat into your greatest multiplier.

Step 1: Identify the Adversary

Name the competitor or industry player you currently spend the most energy defending against or worrying about.

- *My primary competitor/adversary:* ____________

  ____

Step 2: Define the Mutual Gap (the Free Zone Opportunity)

Collaboration requires complementary capabilities. Analyze the strengths and weaknesses objectively.

- *What unique capability or asset do they possess that I lack?* (e.g., distribution, specific technology, market access, specialized talent)
    - *Their strength:* ________________________

      ____
- *What unique capability or asset do I possess that they lack?* (e.g., proprietary IP, operational excellence, brand credibility, specific expertise)
    - *My strength:* __________________________

      ____
- *Example: Dale Wills had development expertise; the banks had capital and distressed assets.*

Step 3: Define the Exponential Value (the 1+1=11 Equation)

If you combined your strengths, what new market, platform, or standard could you create together?

- *The exponential value we could create:*

  ____

  ____
- *Example: Marc Benioff created AppExchange, transforming competitors into contributors on his platform.*

Step 4: The First Move (the Outreach)

Courage precedes collaboration. Draft the opening line of the e-mail or phone call you will make this week to propose this exploration.

- *My opening line: ______________________________*

  ____

  ____

- *Example: "We've been competing fiercely for years. I have a proposal for how we might build something together that neither of us could achieve alone."*

The Scorecard: Measure Your Community

Quantify your current ecosystem architecture. Score yourself from 1 (zero-sum thinking) to 12 (ecosystem architect) in each category:

Category	Description	Now (1–12)	12-Month Target
Abundance Architecture	I view business as positive-sum value creation.	___	___
Strategic Generosity	I systematically share frameworks to strengthen the ecosystem.	___	___
Competitor Collaboration	I actively partner with "competitors" for multiplication.	___	___
Platform Building	I architect systems that enable industry transformation.	___	___
Ecosystem Investment	I invest time and resources in strengthening the business environment.	___	___
Multiplier Network	I am surrounded by decade-thinking entrepreneurs.	___	___
TOTAL SCORE:		___/ 72	

Score Interpretation:

- **6–30:** Trapped in zero-sum thinking (the 94.6% trap)
- **31–50:** Beginning to see multiplication opportunities
- **51–72:** Architecting ecosystems (the 5.4% zone)

THE DASHBOARD INTEGRATION: ARCHITECT YOUR ECOSYSTEM

Your Competitor-to-Collaborator Shift and Scorecard provide the data required to move from isolation to multiplication.

Scan the QR code below or go to TheGreaterGameDashboard.com and input your Greater Community score.

Here's how the platform empowers your ecosystem strategy:

1. **The Ecosystem Benchmark:** Entrepreneurial Pulse data reveals how the top 5.4% leverage ecosystems. Benchmark your collaboration score against the 37.1% of $50+ million entrepreneurs who actively co-create solutions—versus the 10.1% who remain isolated.

2. **The Command Center View:** Your Greater Community score integrates into your overall GMI (greater multipliers index), revealing how your relationship architecture accelerates or limits growth across all other multipliers. Collaboration is the gateway to exponential scale.
3. **Your Recommended Actions:** Based on your ecosystem architecture, the platform surfaces personalized pathways:
   - **VFO Second Opinion**—If your isolation stems from wealth complexity that competitors might exploit, this pathway builds the protective structures that enable confident collaboration.
   - **Strategic Coach Acceleration**—If you're trapped in zero-sum thinking, this pathway connects you with decade-thinking entrepreneurs who model abundance architecture.

What if your biggest competitor became your greatest multiplier? Activate your dashboard and start the conversation now.

CHAPTER 6

GREATER TEAMWORK—FROM MANAGING PEOPLE TO MULTIPLYING GENIUS

While others exhaust themselves managing employees, you're architecting self-managing leaders who multiply your vision without your presence.

THE 600-PERSON PRISON YOU BUILT FOR YOURSELF

You're calculating the compounding cost of being irreplaceable.

Six hundred employees; 180 resignations per year. Every Monday, another wave of exits. Every crisis requires a call to your personal cell. Every decision creates a bottleneck with your name on it.

The math is crushing you: If you step away for two weeks, revenue drops 20%. If you're gone for a month, operations start to fail. If you were to disappear for three months, the entire enterprise would collapse.

You've built a $60 million prison where you're simultaneously the warden, the architect, and the only inmate who can't leave.

Meanwhile, the competitor you've been watching—the one with half your headcount—just sold for 12x EBITDA while the founder worked 25 hours a week. Their secret? They stopped managing people and started multiplying leaders.

Here's what's destroying you at 2:47 A.M.: Your family doesn't know the person you've become. Your spouse has stopped asking about your day because it's always about managing problems, not building dreams. That vacation you promised? Canceled again because "no one else can handle this."

You've built the foundation (Stage 1). You've engineered the energy (Stage 2). You've started architecting the ecosystem (Chapter 5). But here's the brutal truth: All that potential remains trapped if you are the organizational bottleneck.

The 5.4% who achieve exponential growth have discovered the paradox of leadership: The more you manage, the less you lead. The more you control, the less you scale.

This isn't a management problem; it's an architecture problem. You haven't built a team; you've built a dependency trap.

It's time to stop being the hero who saves the day and become the architect who makes heroes unnecessary.

THE 5.4% INSIGHT: MULTIPLICATION OVER MANAGEMENT

Our Greater Multipliers Study reveals the multiplication divide:

- Among the 5.4%, 38.2% have achieved self-managing teams that run operations independently.
- Among the 94.6%, only 12.7% reach this level—while roughly half empower leaders with some autonomy, they haven't crossed into true self-management.

The critical distinction: Empowerment isn't enough. The 5.4% build teams that don't just execute autonomously—they innovate and multiply without the founder present.

The data confirms what you already know: Your involvement is costing you growth.

THE INDISPENSABILITY DISCOUNT: THE VALUATION COST OF YOUR INVOLVEMENT

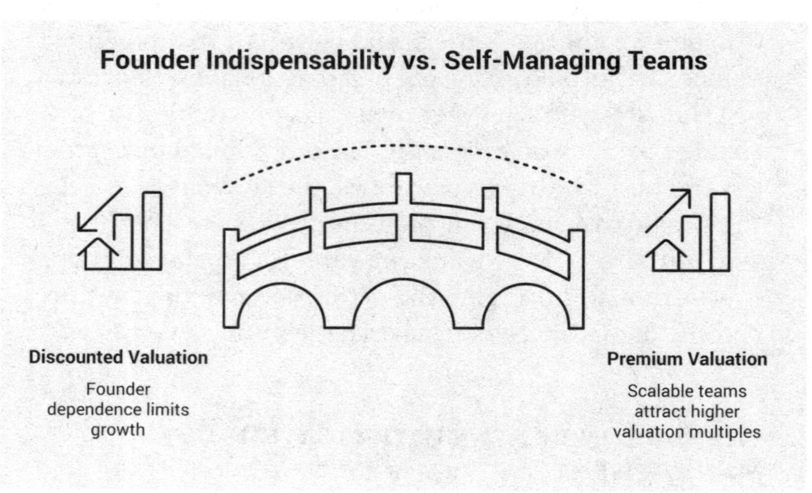

Private equity buyers quantify this dependency. They refer to it as the indispensability discount.

- **Founder-Dependent (the 94.6% Trap):** 3–5x EBITDA, high turnover, slow decision-making, and limited scalability
- **Self-Managing Teams (the 5.4% Zone):** 10–15x EBITDA, low turnover, agile execution, exponential scalability

On a $10 million EBITDA business, that's the difference between a $40 million exit and a $120 million exit. Your indispensability is costing you $80 million.

THE DELEGATION DELUSION VERSUS THE EMPOWERMENT REALITY

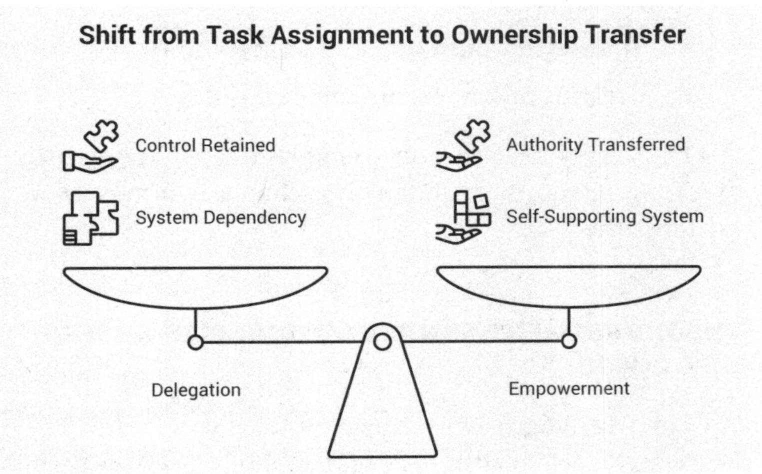

The 94.6% try to solve this problem with better management systems, more rigorous delegation, and tighter controls. They believe more growth requires more personal effort. This path leads only to exhaustion and stagnation.

The delegation delusion traps them.

DELEGATION (THE 94.6% TRAP):

- Assigning unwanted tasks
- Dictating the "how"
- Maintaining control and responsibility
- Creating dependency and bottlenecks

The 5.4% operate from the reality of empowerment.

EMPOWERMENT (THE 5.4% ZONE):

- Granting ownership of essential outcomes
- Defining the "what" and the "why"
- Transferring authority and responsibility
- Creating autonomy and multiplication

The shift from delegation to empowerment is the essence of scaling. It requires a fundamental change in mindset and architecture.

THE INVESTMENT MINDSET: PEOPLE AS ASSETS, NOT COSTS

The shift begins with how you view your team. The 94.6% see people as costs to be managed. The 5.4% see them as assets to be multiplied.

As Jennifer Borislow (Chapter 2) demonstrated, investing in human capital isn't just an operational strategy; it's a foundational security measure. "It's the people around me that give me the security and confidence to aim higher," she says.

When you view people as investments, you focus on maximizing their return, not minimizing their cost. You invest in their growth, their development, and their potential.

MIKE WANDLER: THE 600-TO-250 TRANSFORMATION

Mike Wandler was trapped in the 600-person prison. His company L&H Industrial was growing, but so was the complexity, the turnover, and the exhaustion.

"I was working 80-hour weeks just to keep the lights on," Wandler recalls. "I realized I hadn't built a business; I had built a machine that consumed me."

Through Strategic Coach, Mike discovered what kills 94.6% of successful entrepreneurs: **The problem wasn't the people. The problem was the game.**

"I realized I wasn't developing leaders. I was creating dependents. Every 'helpful' answer I gave was stealing someone's opportunity to grow."

Wandler made a radical decision: He stopped managing people and started multiplying genius.

The Multiplication Architecture:

- **The organizational redesign:** He restructured the company around small, autonomous teams focused on specific outcomes.
- **The Unique Ability focus:** He implemented Strategic Coach's Unique Ability framework, ensuring everyone operated in their zone of genius.

- **The empowerment protocol:** He shifted from dictating processes to defining outcomes and granting freedom of execution.

The Exponential Results:

- **People impact:**
    - Headcount: 600 → 250 (58% reduction)
    - Performance: doubled output with half the staff
- **Financial impact:**
    - Revenue: from $60 million to $120 million (2x growth)
    - Net margins: from 15.4% to 24%
    - Valuation: from 3x to 8x EBITDA multiple
- **Freedom impact:**
    - Owner hours: from 70 hours to 25 hours weekly
    - Innovation: new opportunities emerged spontaneously

The multiplication paradox: Half the headcount, twice the results—because 250 people using their Unique Ability outperform 600 managing bureaucracy.

KENT PILCHER: THE ARCHITECTURE OF EMPOWERMENT

While Wandler focused on organizational redesign, Kent Pilcher demonstrates how to institutionalize empowerment through precise frameworks and a cultural operating system.

Pilcher's real estate firm was successful but stagnant. Growth required his direct involvement in every transaction, every decision, every crisis.

"I was the bottleneck," Pilcher admits. "I realized I needed to stop being the smartest person in the room and start building a room full of smart people."

Pilcher architected a system for systematic empowerment.

THE EMPOWERMENT FRAMEWORK: OUTCOME CLARITY, METHOD FREEDOM

Pilcher implemented a simple yet profound framework: Define the outcome but grant freedom in the method.

- **Outcome clarity (the "what" and the "why"):** Define what success looks like and why it matters.
- **Method freedom (the "how"):** Empower the team to choose the path to the outcome.
- **Success metrics (the measurement):** Define how success will be measured.

This shift transformed the organization. Team members stopped asking, "How do you want me to do this?" and started saying, "Here's how I'm going to achieve this."

THE CULTURAL OPERATING SYSTEM: PERFORMANCE ATTITUDES

Pilcher knew that frameworks alone weren't enough. He needed a cultural operating system that reinforced empowerment and autonomy. He defined four performance attitudes that became the foundation of the culture:

- **Alert:** Aware of opportunities and threats
- **Curious:** Seeking understanding and innovation
- **Responsive:** Acting quickly and decisively
- **Resourceful:** Finding solutions despite constraints

These attitudes shifted the focus from compliance to creativity, from following orders to achieving outcomes.

The Exponential Results:

- **Workforce:** from 80 to 400 employees (5x growth)
- **Geographic scale:** from one office to eight offices across five states
- **Transaction volume:** 10x increase
- **Founder focus:** from 100% operational to 94.6% strategy and relationships
- **Time freedom:** from 14 vacation days to more than 100 days for family and strategic thinking

The multiplication effect: Pilcher didn't just scale operations—he architected a self-managing organization where leadership multiplies at every level without his involvement.

THE UNIQUE ABILITY MULTIPLIER: THE ENGINE OF GENIUS

The foundation of greater teamwork is ensuring everyone operates within their Unique Ability—the intersection of their greatest passion and their greatest talent.

The 94.6% hire people to fill roles. The 5.4% hire people to leverage their Unique Ability.

THE BARTERING SYSTEM: TRADING TASKS FOR UNIQUE ABILITY

The 5.4% implement a bartering system, where team members trade tasks to align with their Unique Ability.

- **Identify generators and drains:** Use the energy audit discussed in Chapter 3.
- **Trade the drains:** Delegate or trade tasks that drain energy and fall outside Unique Ability.
- **Maximize the generators:** Focus time and effort on tasks that generate energy and leverage Unique Ability.

This system ensures that the organization operates at peak energy and efficiency, maximizing the collective genius of the team.

THE MULTIPLICATION ARCHITECTURE BLUEPRINT: HOW TO BUILD YOUR SELF-MANAGING TEAM

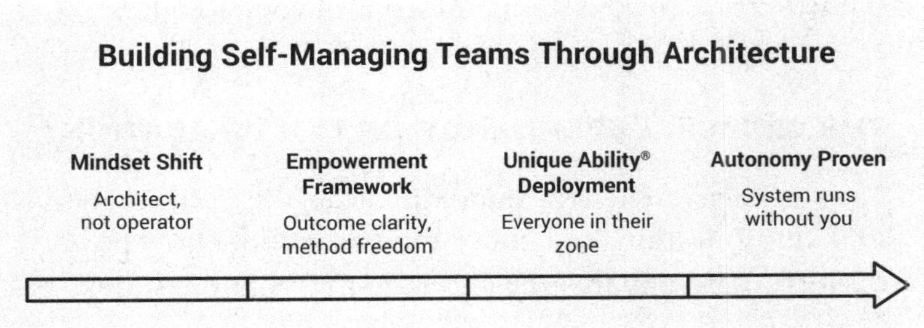

The 5.4% don't rely on charisma; they rely on architecture. Here is the four-phase blueprint for building your self-managing team.

Phase 1: The Mindset Shift (from Management to Multiplication)

Adopt the investment mindset. Commit to the shift from delegation to empowerment. Define your role as the architect, not the operator.

Phase 2: The Framework Implementation (the Tools of Empowerment)

Implement the Empowerment Framework (Outcome Clarity, Method Freedom). Define the performance attitudes that will govern your culture.

Phase 3: The Unique Ability Deployment (the Engine of Genius)

Implement the Unique Ability framework and the bartering system. Ensure everyone is operating in their unique ability.

Phase 4: The Autonomy Test (the Proof of Multiplication)

Systematically test the self-managing architecture. Take autonomy baby steps (as we will explore in Chapter 7). Gradually increase the duration and scope of your absence.

THE CHOICE: DEPENDENCY OR MULTIPLICATION?

You have reached the midpoint of Stage 3: Collaboration and Multiplication. You understand the exponential power of shifting from managing people to multiplying genius.

The choice is now yours: Will you continue to be the bottleneck, constrained by your own capacity and trapped in the 600-person prison? Or will you become the architect, building a self-managing organization that multiplies your vision without your presence?

Will you settle for the indispensability discount (3–5x)? Or will you command the multiplication premium (10–15x)?

THE BRIDGE TO GREATER AUTONOMY

Greater teamwork is the prerequisite for the final step of Stage 3: Greater Autonomy. When you build a self-managing team, you unlock the freedom to focus on your highest-value activities—vision, strategy, and innovation.

In Chapter 7, Collaboration and Multiplication, you will discover how to transform this organizational independence into personal freedom. You will learn how to move from indispensable to invincible, architecting a life where your presence is optional, but your impact is exponential.

It's time to engineer your freedom.

ACTIVATE YOUR FOCUS MULTIPLIER

THE BRIDGE: FROM MANAGEMENT TO MULTIPLICATION

You've recognized the 600-person prison, realizing that that you haven't built an organization; you've built an elaborate dependency trap where every decision requires your approval.

The 94.6% try to solve this with better management systems, more rigorous delegation, and tighter controls. They believe more growth requires more personal effort. This path leads only to exhaustion, high turnover, and a valuation multiple that reflects your indispensability (3–5x).

The 5.4%, like Mike Wandler and Kent Pilcher, discovered the multiplication formula: Stop managing people and start multiplying genius. They shifted from delegation (assigning unwanted tasks) to empowerment (trusting others with essential outcomes). They focused everyone on their Unique Ability and cultivated performance attitudes. This path leads to self-managing teams, exponential growth, and true freedom (10–15x multiples).

It's time to stop being the hero who saves the day and become the architect who makes heroes unnecessary.

THE MULTIPLIER ACTIVATION: THE EMPOWERMENT INVERSION

This exercise is designed to initiate the crucial shift from delegation to empowerment. You will transform one recurring task into an autonomous outcome, starting this Monday.

Step 1: Identify the Delegated Task (the Bottleneck)

Identify one significant task or process you currently delegate where you still dictate the "how." This is something where you frequently check in, correct the methodology, or remain the final approval point.

- *The task I currently micromanage:* ________________

  ____

- *Examples: Quarterly investor reporting, new client onboarding process, weekly sales pipeline review.*

Step 2: Define the Empowered Outcome (the Shift)

Reframe the task using Kent Pilcher's architecture: Outcome Clarity, Method Freedom. Define the "what" and the "why" but explicitly eliminate the "how."

- *The desired outcome (what success looks like):*

  ____

- *The strategic importance (why it matters):*

  ____

- *The success metrics (how we will measure it):*

  ____

Step 3: The Handoff (the Liberation)

Communicate the new structure to the responsible team member by this Monday. Use this specific language:

- *"I want to empower you to own this outcome. Here is what success looks like and why it matters [share Step 2]. How you achieve it is entirely up to you. I trust your judgment. Let's schedule a check-in [on date], not for approval but to confirm we have shared clarity on the outcome."*

Step 4: The Commitment to Silence (the Hardest Part)

Commit to not intervening in the "how," even if they do it differently than you would. When they ask you how to do it, your response must be: "What do you think is the best approach?"

The Scorecard: Measure Your Teamwork

Quantify your current multiplication architecture. Score yourself from 1 (dependency trap) to 12 (true multiplication) in each category:

Category	Description	Now (1–12)	12-Month Target
Language Revolution	I use "empower," not "delegate," and "team members," not "employees."	___	___
Investment Mindset	I view people as appreciating assets, not costs.	___	___
Outcome Clarity	I define the "what" and let my team own the "how."	___	___
Method Freedom	I give my teams freedom to choose their path to outcomes.	___	___
Unique Ability Deployment	I ensure everyone operates in their Unique Ability.	___	___
Performance Attitudes	I cultivate an Alert, Curious, Responsive, Resourceful culture.	___	___
Cascade Multiplication	I develop leaders who create leaders at every level.	___	___
Self-Management Reality	My business runs without me.	___	___
Innovation Rate	Ideas emerge without my involvement.	___	___
Strategic Focus	I spend 90%+ of my time on vision, not operations.	___	___
TOTAL SCORE:		___ / 120	

Score Interpretation:

- **10–40:** Dependency trap (you are the bottleneck; high CQS likely)
- **41–80:** Beginning multiplication (freedom emerging)
- **81–120:** True multiplication (the 5.4% zone)

THE DASHBOARD INTEGRATION: MULTIPLY YOUR LEADERS

Your Empowerment Inversion and Scorecard reveal exactly where your operational bottlenecks are. This isn't just about efficiency; it's about unlocking scale.

Scan the QR code below or go to TheGreaterGameDashboard.com and input your Greater Teamwork score.

Here's how the platform translates this data into action:

1. **The Multiplication Benchmark:** Your greater teamwork score reveals how much your current team architecture depends on you versus multiplies without you. Compare your score against the 25.8% of $50+ million entrepreneurs who have achieved fully self-managing teams, as identified in the Entrepreneurial Pulse research.

2. **The Command Center View:** Your teamwork score integrates into your overall GMI (greater multipliers index), quantifying the impact of operational bottlenecks and founder dependency on your multiplication potential across all other multipliers.
3. **Your Recommended Actions:** Based on your team architecture, the platform surfaces personalized pathways:
   - **VFO Second Opinion**—If team bottlenecks stem from compensation complexity, equity structures, or key-person risk, this pathway addresses the wealth architecture that enables confident delegation.
   - **Strategic Coach Acceleration**—If founder dependence is your primary constraint, this pathway provides the execution frameworks to build leaders who create leaders at every level.

If you disappeared for three months, would your business thrive or falter? Activate your dashboard and start multiplying now.

CHAPTER 7

GREATER AUTONOMY—FROM INDISPENSABLE TO INVINCIBLE

While others build prisons disguised as empires, you're architecting freedom that multiplies value in your absence.

THE HURRICANE THAT PROVED EVERYTHING

August 2017. Hurricane Irma, a Category 5 monster, bears down on Necker Island.

Richard Branson hunkers in his wine cellar with family and staff, completely cut off from the outside world. No power. No communications. His private island—his home and headquarters for decades—is about to be devastated.

The Virgin empire should be paralyzed: Critical decisions on hold. Deals frozen. Operations stumbling.

Instead, Virgin Atlantic closed a £200 million refinancing. Virgin Galactic advanced its spacecraft testing. Virgin Hotels opened a new property. Across more than 400 Virgin companies, not a single critical decision waited for Branson's input.

When Branson emerged days later, he discovered that his businesses didn't just survive—they thrived. Revenue was up across multiple divisions. Three new partnerships were signed. Innovation continued.

As Branson later reflected, the hurricane forced the ultimate test: Could Virgin exist without him? The answer was better than yes—the business was stronger without him hovering over every decision.

THE INDISPENSABILITY TRAP

Let's be honest about where you are right now.

Your phone buzzes at 2:47 A.M. It's not a hurricane; it's a solvable operational issue that somehow requires your personal intervention. Again.

You've built the foundation (Stage 1). You've engineered the energy (Stage 2). You've architected the ecosystem (Chapter 5) and empowered the team (Chapter 6).

Yet, you remain the indispensable bottleneck. The critical path. The single point of failure.

You're exhausted not by the work but by the weight of being needed. Your family misses you even when you're home. That sabbatical you promised yourself? Postponed indefinitely because "the timing isn't right."

Here's the brutal truth: If your business can't thrive without you, you don't own an asset; you own a job. You haven't built an empire; you've built a dependency trap.

The 94.6% wear their 80-hour workweeks and constant availability as badges of honor. They believe being needed for every decision is proof of their value. In reality, it's proof of their failure to architect systems that multiply without them.

The illusion of indispensability traps them.

The 5.4% understand the ultimate paradox of the Greater Game: Your presence is a multiplier, but your absence is exponential.

They don't achieve freedom through heroic effort; they achieve it through systematic design. They engineer businesses that continue to grow even after they're gone.

THE 5.4% INSIGHT: AUTONOMY AS THE ULTIMATE ASSET

Our Greater Multipliers Study reveals the impact of autonomy on enterprise value:

- Among the 5.4% achieving exponential growth, 47.3% are free from daily operations, focusing only on strategic breakthroughs.
- These autonomous entrepreneurs command significantly higher valuation multiples (10–15x+) compared to their indispensable peers (3–5x).

Autonomy isn't a reward you earn after decades of sacrifice; it's the architecture you build today.

THE VALUATION EVIDENCE: THE INDISPENSABILITY DISCOUNT REVISITED

As discussed in Chapter 6, the market penalizes founder dependency. The "indispensability discount" is the price you pay for being irreplaceable.

- **Indispensable (the 94.6% trap):** The EBITDA is 3–5x. Your presence is required for operations.

- **Invincible (the 5.4% zone):** The EBITDA is 15x+. Your presence is optional; the architecture runs the business.

On a $10 million EBITDA business, that's the difference between a $40 million exit and a $150 million exit. Your indispensability is costing you $110 million.

Autonomy isn't a lifestyle choice; it's a strategic imperative.

THE AUTONOMY LADDER: THE PROGRESSION FROM HOSTAGE TO CREATOR

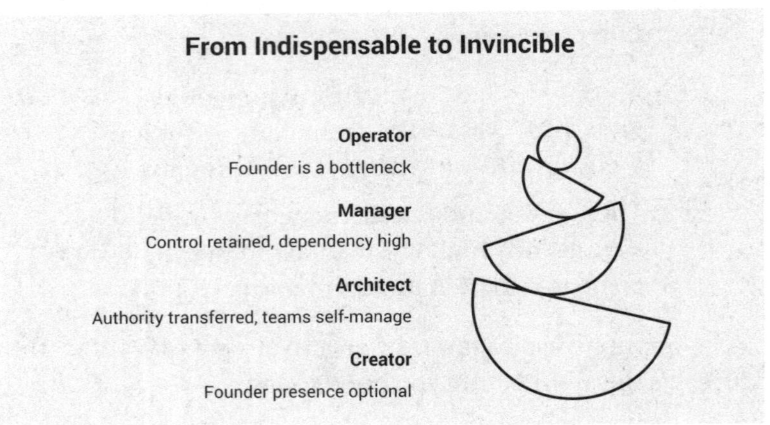

The journey from indispensable to invincible follows a predictable progression: the Autonomy Ladder. Where are you standing right now?

Rung 1: The Operator (the 94.6% Trap)

- **The reality:** You are the business. Every decision requires your approval; you work 80+ hour weeks. There is constant firefighting.

- **The constraint:** your time and energy
- **The valuation:** 3–5x EBITDA

Rung 2: The Manager (the Optimization Zone)

- **The reality:** You manage people who execute tasks. Delegation, not empowerment. You work 60+ hour weeks. Operational bottlenecks remain.
- **The constraint:** your management capacity
- **The valuation:** 6–8x EBITDA

Rung 3: The Architect (the 5.4% Zone)

- **The reality:** You design systems and empower leaders. You have self-managing teams; you work 30–40-hour workweeks. Strategic focus.
- **The constraint:** the quality of your architecture
- **The valuation:** 10–15x EBITDA

Rung 4: The Creator (the Exponential Zone)

- **The reality:** You create new games and architect new ecosystems. Your presence is optional; you work 10–20-hour weeks (on this business). Infinite scalability.
- **The constraint:** your vision and ambition
- **The valuation:** 15–30x+ EBITDA

The goal isn't to climb the ladder; it's to build the architecture that makes the climb inevitable.

GINO WICKMAN: ARCHITECTING THE ABSENCE THAT MULTIPLIES

The Autonomy Ladder illustrates the changes that occur at each level. Gino Wickman demonstrates how, through systematic removal, he increased both fidelity and scale.

By 28, Gino Wickman was exhausted from co-owning (with a one-third stake) and running his family business. The operational chaos was crushing him. But that crucible forged something profound: a passion for helping entrepreneurs achieve their business goals. This singular drive would fuel his transformation from overwhelmed operator to the architect of a system that runs without him.

Over 20 years, Wickman personally worked with 135 clients, extracting and refining the patterns that would become the Entrepreneurial Operating System (EOS). But he faced the calculation that would define his autonomy journey: "I could help 200 companies in my lifetime, or I could help 10,000."

Most experts would have built a premium consulting practice, trading their time for increasingly higher fees. Wickman saw the trap—and designed his way out of it.

THE FIVE-YEAR FREEDOM ARCHITECTURE

Wickman's genius wasn't just creating EOS—it was architecting his complete removal from its delivery. This wasn't an accident or a sudden decision; it was a methodical five-year plan to build a leadership team and transition into the owner's role.

"I built a strong leadership team," Wickman explains, "so I was planning on sitting in that owner's box and letting this leadership team grow the company."

This is the crucial distinction that separates the 5.4% from everyone else: Wickman wasn't positioning for an exit—he was architecting for freedom. The difference is profound:

- **Positioning for exit** by building to sell, often compromising long-term value for short-term metrics
- **Architecting for freedom** by building systems so robust that your presence becomes optional

Partnering with Don Tinney to form EOS Worldwide, Wickman didn't just delegate; he eliminated himself through systematic multiplication.

THE MULTIPLICATION ARCHITECTURE:

- **Rigorous certification process** to ensure fidelity without his involvement
- **Standardized tools** (V/TO, accountability chart, GWC, etc.) that work identically everywhere
- **Training infrastructure** to transform consultants into multipliers of his methodology
- **Quality systems** to maintain consistency across implementations globally

This is the blueprint for genuine autonomy: Create systems so comprehensive that anyone trained in them can deliver your methodology with precision.

THE UNEXPECTED VALIDATION

In May 2018, something unexpected happened that proved his architecture worked.

Someone made an offer for EOS Worldwide.

Wickman's response reveals his mindset: "Are you kidding me? Is that what it's worth?"

The valuation came in at almost a 10x multiple—a number that validates the power of systematic removal. He sold 87.5%, retaining 12.5% ownership in the company he'd architected to thrive without him.

At the time of sale, 200 certified implementers were spreading EOS. Today, 850 implementers serve 300,000+ companies globally—and Wickman hasn't personally implemented EOS in years.

The transformation metrics tell the story of multiplication beyond presence:

- **Personal delivery:** 135 clients over 20 years
- **Multiplied delivery:** 300,000+ companies running on EOS
- **Time freedom:** complete operational independence
- **Valuation:** a multiple that validated the power of letting go

THE ABSENCE MULTIPLIER IN ACTION

When you visit the EOS Worldwide website today, Wickman's picture is notably absent from most pages. Thousands of businesses are being transformed this week by tools Wickman hasn't touched in years, through implementers Wickman has never met.

Most experts fear that packaging their expertise makes them obsolete. Wickman proved the opposite: The more systematically you give away your expertise, the more valuable you become. He didn't just escape the trap of being indispensable to his own success—he turned it into a launching pad for exponential impact at multiple levels.

THE CASCADING FREEDOM

Here's where Wickman demonstrates the ultimate expression of greater autonomy: using freedom to create more freedom at entirely new levels.

Post-sale, Wickman didn't retire. He launched two new ventures:

- **Entrepreneurial Leap:** targeting early-stage entrepreneurs to help them discover whether they're wired for entrepreneurship
- **Shine:** supporting driven entrepreneurs in finding inner peace—particularly those who've sold their businesses and feel empty despite their "success"

But Wickman's most profound insight transcends any single venture. He discovered a pattern in his own journey—a systematic progression of turning competition into collaboration that compounds autonomy at each level.

Level 1: "I was an entrepreneur competing with all these other entrepreneurs. So, I decided to help entrepreneurs and turned the very entrepreneurs I was competing with into my clients."

Level 2: "Then I decided to assist individuals who are interested in supporting entrepreneurs. So, I turned all those consultants and coaches that were working with entrepreneurs—that I competed with—into my clients by allowing them to license the system."

Each elevation not only reduced competition but also exponentially multiplied impact while increasing autonomy. The same man who, at 28, was exhausted co-owning and running his family business now has:

- A methodology transforming 300,000+ companies globally
- Two new ventures creating impact at different life stages
- Complete time freedom to pursue what matters most
- A business model that generates value while he sleeps

This is the absence multiplier in its purest form: architecture so robust that growth accelerates without you—freeing you to create what's next.

EVAN RYAN: THE 300-DAY ABSENCE MULTIPLIER

Detailed in his work on scaling technology companies, Evan Ryan achieved what most entrepreneurs consider impossible: He traveled the world for 300 days while his company grew 3x.

Ryan's software company was successful, but he was trapped on Rung 1—The Operator. He was indispensable, exhausted, and constrained.

He made the conscious decision to architect his freedom.

THE AUTONOMY ARCHITECTURE:

- **The dashboard system:** He built a real-time dashboard that tracked every critical metric, eliminating the need for constant check-ins.
- **The leadership blueprint:** He empowered his leadership team with clear decision-making frameworks and full authority (as discussed in Chapter 6).
- **The communication protocol:** He established a structured communication cadence (weekly strategic meetings, monthly reviews) that maximized clarity and minimized noise.

THE EXPONENTIAL RESULTS:

- **Location freedom:** 300 days traveling annually
- **Revenue growth:** 3x increase during his absence
- **Team innovation:** launched new products and markets autonomously
- **Crisis interruptions:** fewer than five calls per year
- **Strategic focus:** 80% of working hours on vision
- **Life design:** "Living my exact ideal life."

TIM FERRISS: THE ARCHITECTURE OF LIBERATION

While Evan Ryan focused on organizational autonomy, Tim Ferriss demonstrates how to architect personal liberation through systematic elimination, automation, and outsourcing.

Ferriss's book, *The 4-Hour Workweek*, became a cultural phenomenon not because it promised laziness, but because it offered a blueprint for maximizing impact while minimizing effort.

The Liberation Architecture:

- **The 80/20 principle:** Identify the 20% of activities generating 80% of results; eliminate the rest ruthlessly.
- **Parkinson's law:** Set aggressive deadlines to force focused execution.
- **Automation and outsourcing:** Leverage technology and global talent to handle repetitive tasks and non-core functions.

The Exponential Results:

- **Time freedom:** from 80 hours to 4 hours per week (on his primary business)
- **Income growth:** 12x increase in income
- **Impact expansion:** used freedom to become a best-selling author, investor, and thought leader

Ferriss didn't just optimize his time; he revolutionized the relationship between effort and impact, proving that autonomy is accessible regardless of scale.

BETH KRASZEWSKI: THE AUTONOMY BABY STEPS

As she describes in her autonomy journey, wealth manager Beth Kraszewski demonstrates how small, intentional steps build toward invincibility.

A self-described "recovering type A" personality, Kraszewski used to exert control over every aspect of her practice. "Entrepreneurs just know how to get stuff done, which of course means we think we should be trying to do all the stuff!" says Kraszewski, founder of Chicago-based Purposeful Wealth Advisers.

A health scare and the birth of her children forced her to see the importance of building a self-managing team and systematizing processes. "Systems are absolutely needed to create sustainability and scalability within a company," she says.

To put the team and systems to the test, Kraszewski took "autonomy baby steps."

The Systematic Testing:

- **The closed door:** closing her door to visitors during certain times of the day
- **The unplugged walk:** going for walks without her phone
- **The 48-hour disappearance:** taking short breaks to test the systems

She found that the firm operated well during those times, and she herself was more productive and creative.

Those baby steps eventually led to bigger leaps—including taking extended time off and traveling.

She spends the bulk of her time on strategic initiatives, while the team handles day-to-day operations.

"I am not needed in the office for the company to thrive," she says. "In fact, the company is more successful when I am not there because it forces the team to step up and take ownership."

"Autonomy is not about checking out," she says. "It's about checking in to what matters most."

THE MYTHS OF AUTONOMY (AND HOW TO DISMANTLE THEM)

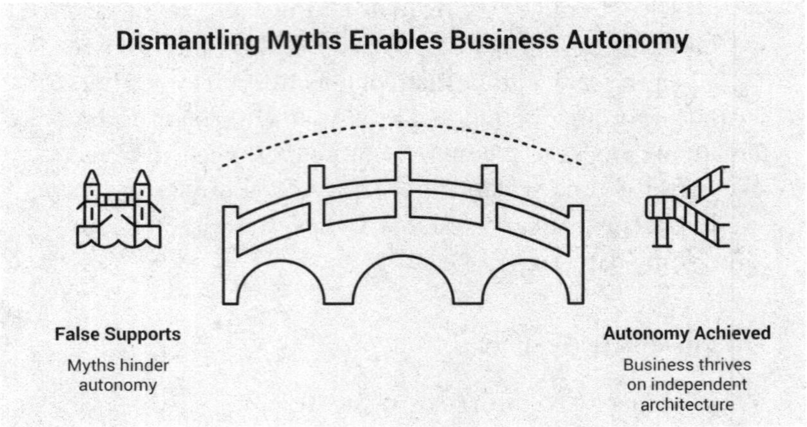

Four myths keep 94.6% of people ensnared in the indispensability trap.

Myth 1: I can't let go. (They'll screw it up.)

Reality: If your team can't execute without you, it's not their failure; it's your architectural failure. You haven't established the systems, frameworks, or culture necessary for autonomy.

Wickman's response: Build certification systems so rigorous that anyone trained in them can deliver your methodology with precision.

Myth 2: Autonomy means abdication. (I'll lose control.)

Reality: Autonomy isn't about losing control; it's about shifting control from personal oversight to systemic architecture. Dashboards, metrics, and clear frameworks provide more control than micromanagement ever could.

Ryan's proof: His dashboard system provided him with more visibility into global operations than he had when working from the office.

Myth 3: I'll become irrelevant. (What will I do?)

Reality: Autonomy frees you to focus on your highest-value activities—vision, strategy, innovation, and creating new games. You move from operator to creator.

Wickman's evidence: Freedom to launch Entrepreneurial Leap and Shine—entirely new ventures that wouldn't have been possible while trapped in EOS operations.

Myth 4: It's too late. (I'm already trapped.)

Reality: Autonomy is an architectural project, not a personality transplant. You can start building it today, one system, one framework, one autonomy baby step at a time.

Kraszewski's journey: From controlling every detail to working remotely in a different state—built through incremental baby steps.

THE AUTONOMY ARCHITECTURE BLUEPRINT: HOW TO ENGINEER YOUR FREEDOM

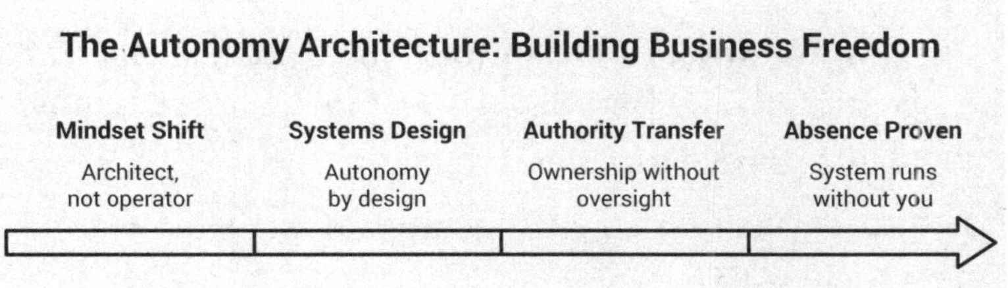

The 5.4% don't hope for freedom; they engineer it. Here is the four-phase blueprint for achieving greater autonomy.

Phase 1: The Mindset Shift (from Indispensable to Invincible)

Commit to the goal of making yourself unnecessary. Embrace the absence multiplier. Recognize that your most significant contribution is the architecture, not the operation.

Wickman's framework: A methodical five-year plan with a clear destination—the owner's box.

Phase 2: The Systems Design (the Architecture of Freedom)

Build the systems that enable autonomy:

- Implement the dashboard system (Evan Ryan)
- Leverage liberation architecture (Tim Ferriss)
- Codify your IP into standardized tools (Wickman)
- Create certification processes that ensure fidelity (Wickman)

Phase 3: The Authority Transfer (the Empowerment Engine)

Implement the empowerment framework (Chapter 6). Empower your leadership team with apparent decision-making authority and ownership of outcomes.

Wickman's leadership team was so capable that when an unexpected acquisition offer arrived, the company was already architected to thrive without him.

Phase 4: The Absence Testing (the Proof of Autonomy)

Systematically test the architecture by intentionally removing yourself:

- Start with the autonomy baby steps (Beth Kraszewski)
- Progress to extended absences (Evan Ryan's 300 days)

- Gradually increase the duration and scope of your disappearance

The ultimate test: Can your business grow faster without you than with you?

Wickman's validation: 200 implementers at sale, 850 today—with zero personal involvement from him.

THE CHOICE: HOSTAGE OR CREATOR?

You have completed Stage 3: Collaboration and Multiplication. You have transformed competitors into collaborators (Chapter 5), empowered your team (Chapter 6), and architected your freedom (Chapter 7).

You have achieved what the 94.6% only dream of: a self-managing organization that multiplies without you.

The choice is now yours: Will you remain a hostage to your creation, trapped by the illusion of indispensability? Or will you embrace your role as the creator, using your freedom to design new games and achieve exponential impact?

THE BRIDGE TO STAGE 4: EXPONENTIAL IMPACT

Autonomy is the ultimate liberation. But it is also the ultimate responsibility.

You now have the freedom, the resources, and the energy to play the Greater Game at a level previously unimaginable.

In Stage 4, Exponential Impact, you will discover how to leverage this freedom to create transformative change. You will learn how to shift from reacting to markets to making them (Chapter 8), how to commit to your vision with strategic stubbornness (Chapter 9), and how to transform fear into fuel (Chapter 10).

It's time to move from the freedom from constraint to the freedom to create.

ACTIVATE YOUR TIME MULTIPLIER

THE BRIDGE: FROM INDISPENSABLE TO INVINCIBLE

You have recognized the illusion of indispensability.

The 94.6% wear their 80-hour workweeks and constant availability as badges of honor. They believe being needed for every decision is proof of their value. In reality, it's proof of their failure to architect systems that multiply without them. They are hostages in prisons disguised as empires, ensuring their valuation remains capped (3–5x).

The 5.4% of individuals, like Richard Branson, Gino Wickman, and Evan Ryan, understand the ultimate paradox of the Greater Game: Your presence is a multiplier, but your absence is exponential. They don't achieve freedom through heroic effort; they achieve it through systematic design. They engineer businesses that continue to grow even after they're gone. This is the path to invincibility and valuations exceeding 15x.

Autonomy isn't a reward you earn after decades of sacrifice; it's the architecture you build today. It's time to stop being the bottleneck and start being the architect.

THE MULTIPLIER ACTIVATION: THE 48-HOUR DISAPPEARANCE TEST

This exercise is the ultimate stress test for your architecture. It is designed to reveal exactly where the business depends on you, providing a blueprint for your liberation. If the thought of this exercise terrifies you, you need it more than anyone.

Step 1: Schedule the Absence (the Commitment)

Open your calendar right now. Identify a 48-hour window (two consecutive business days) within the next two weeks. Block it off completely.

- *My disappearance dates:* ______________________

Step 2: Set the Rules of Engagement (the Boundaries)

Autonomy requires absolute boundaries. During these 48 hours:

- No e-mail (autoresponder on, directed to a designated lieutenant)
- No business calls or texts
- No Slack/Teams messages
- No "checking in just to see"

Step 3: Prepare the Team (the Empowerment)

Inform your leadership team. This is not a vacation; it is a systems test. Use this language:

"On [dates], I will be completely unavailable. This is an opportunity for us to test our self-managing architecture. You have full authority to make decisions based on our agreed-upon frameworks. I trust you completely."

(If you do not have a team ready for this, that is your first data point: you have built dependency, not autonomy.)

Step 4: The Absence Audit (the Blueprint)

When you return, do not rush to fix the problems immediately. Conduct a systematic debrief with your leadership team. The items that stalled or broke are not evidence of your team's failure; they are evidence of your architectural gaps.

- *What broke or stalled completely?* (These are the systems you must build next.)

  ____

- *What decisions were escalated that shouldn't have been?* (These require clearer decision frameworks or authority transfer.)

  ____

- *What succeeded or accelerated in your absence?* (This is where multiplication is already happening—amplify it.)

  ____

The Scorecard: Measure Your Autonomy

Quantify your current distance from freedom. Score yourself from 1 (hostage) to 12 (invincible) in each category:

Category	Description	Now (1–12)	12-Month Target
Operational Absence	My business thrives when I'm gone for 30+ days.	___	___
Decision Distribution	I have empowered others to make all operational decisions autonomously.	___	___
Unique Ability Focus	I spend 80%+ of my time on tasks only I can do (vision/strategy).	___	___
Authority Transfer	I have distributed P&L ownership throughout my organization.	___	___

Category	Description	Now (1–12)	12-Month Target
Strategic Freedom	I can pursue any new opportunity immediately, without operational constraints.	___	___
Multiplication Metrics	My company's growth accelerates in my absence.	___	___
	TOTAL SCORE:	___ / 72	

Score Interpretation:

- **6–30:** Hostage to your creation (high CQS likely; significant operational dependency)
- **31–50:** Beginning liberation (systems emerging, but bottlenecks remain)
- **51–72:** True autonomy (the 5.4% zone; presence is optional)

THE DASHBOARD INTEGRATION: ENGINEER YOUR FREEDOM

The results of your 48-Hour Disappearance Test and your Scorecard reveal the actual cost of your involvement and the exact architecture required to make yourself unnecessary.

Scan the QR code below or go to TheGreaterGameDashboard.com and input your Greater Autonomy score.

Here's how the platform operationalizes your path to freedom:

1. **The Indispensability Diagnostic:** Your greater autonomy score reveals exactly how much the

business depends on your daily presence. The platform calculates the gap between your current state and true operational independence—and quantifies the valuation discount you're paying for founder dependency.

2. **The Command Center View:** Your autonomy score integrates into your overall GMI (greater multipliers index), tracking how your personal involvement accelerates or constrains growth across all other multipliers. Benchmark your score against the 47.3% of $50+ million entrepreneurs who have fully stepped back from operations, as tracked by the Entrepreneurial Pulse.
3. **Your Recommended Actions:** Based on your autonomy architecture, the platform surfaces personalized pathways:
    - **VFO Second Opinion**—If your inability to step away stems from wealth concentration or financial complexity that only you understand, this pathway builds the structures that enable confident absence.
    - **Strategic Coach Acceleration**—If founder dependence is operational rather than financial, this pathway provides the frameworks to engineer a business that thrives—and grows faster—without you.

The more irreplaceable you think you are, the less valuable you become. Activate your dashboard and engineer your absence now.

STAGE 4

EXPONENTIAL IMPACT

GREATER AGENCY + GREATER COMMITMENT + GREATER COURAGE

You have the freedom. You have the multiplication. Now discover why the entrepreneurs who change the world are the ones who dare to use their autonomy for audacity.

THE FREEDOM THAT FEELS LIKE A PRISON

2:47 A.M. But this time, it's different.

You're not worried about operations—they run without you. You're not concerned about teams—they multiply without your presence. You're not even thinking about competitors—they've become collaborators in your ecosystem. By every measure of Stage 3, you've achieved the impossible.

Your business grows faster when you're absent than when you're present.

So why does freedom feel so . . . empty?

Why does having infinite options feel more constraining than having none?

Why are you more restless with autonomy than you were with obligations?

Here's the hidden trap of operational freedom: Most entrepreneurs use autonomy for comfort rather than

creation. Autonomy without audacity is just an expensive retirement. Freedom without force is just sophisticated stagnation.

You've become what you fought so hard to achieve: entirely unnecessary for your own success. And it's killing you.

THE THURSDAY MORNING REVELATION

Jensen Huang. NVIDIA. 2006. The gaming business was printing money, running perfectly without his daily involvement. He could have coasted for decades. Instead, he announced they'd bet everything on something that barely existed: AI computing.

Over the next decade, Huang committed more than $12 billion—effectively all of NVIDIA's profits—to building CUDA, a platform for general-purpose GPU computing. The board was stunned. Wall Street was skeptical for years and punished the stock accordingly. But Huang understood what Stage 4 really means: using your freedom to shape the future, not follow it.

He didn't demand a guaranteed return. He didn't set a three-year timeline. He simply believed that the world would eventually need to compute at a scale only NVIDIA could deliver—and he was willing to spend a decade proving it.

The result: A $4.6 trillion market cap at the close of 2025—making NVIDIA the most valuable company on earth at that moment—powering virtually every major AI breakthrough on the planet.

But here's what matters: Huang didn't need to risk everything. He chose to. That's the difference between Stage 3 and Stage 4.

THE SUCCESS THAT BECOMES YOUR CRISIS

You've mastered Stage 3:

- Your competitors collaborate in your ecosystem.
- Your team self-manages and multiplies your vision.
- Your presence is optional, your absence profitable.
- Your time is entirely yours.

Last week, you took a month off. Revenue increased 12%. Your team launched three initiatives you hadn't even imagined. Your ecosystem partners closed deals you didn't know existed.

You should be celebrating. Instead, you're calculating.

Because you've discovered the terrifying truth that only the 5.4% understand: **When you're no longer needed, you must decide why you're necessary.**

THE CAUTIONARY TALE OF THE COMFORTABLE

Remember Blockbuster's CEO in 2004? Complete operational autonomy. Nine thousand stores are running perfectly—$5.9 billion in revenue on autopilot.

He used his freedom to optimize. To protect. To coast.

Meanwhile, Netflix used its power to transform an industry.

By 2010, Blockbuster was bankrupt—not because they lacked freedom, but because they lacked the courage to use it for transformation.

That's the hidden trap of Stage 3 success: The moment you achieve perfect autonomy is the moment you're most vulnerable to disruption.

Path A: The Comfortable Decline (the Common Choice)

- Use autonomy for leisure and lifestyle.
- Optimize existing success incrementally.
- Protect what you've built defensively.
- Become a wealthy irrelevance.

Path B: The Exponential Explosion (the Courageous Choice)

- Use autonomy for audacious creation.
- Architect new markets entirely.
- Risk everything on invisible futures.
- Become an industry revolutionary.

Among entrepreneurs worth more than $50 million who've achieved autonomy:

- Only 34.8% use freedom to create new industry standards.
- Just 28.1% maintain unwavering commitment, where every decision stems from a deeply ingrained long-term perspective.
- The paradox: While 39.3% view failure as vital for breakthroughs, only 28.1% actively embrace significant risks.

The shocking truth: Most entrepreneurs intellectually understand risk but emotionally avoid it. The 5.4% close that gap.

THE THREE FORCES THAT CREATE INDUSTRY TRANSFORMATION (AND WHY THIS SEQUENCE MATTERS)

Freedom without these three forces—in this specific order—is just early retirement with extra steps.

First: greater agency (Chapter 8). You must create the new market before committing to it. The agency provides you with the vision and architecture to transform industries. You'll discover how Mark Young turned dead pharmacy machines into a media empire with 3 million daily viewers in 18 months and how Carter Froelich's Launch Bonds eliminated seven-year waiting periods, creating $2 billion in value in just two years. **Without greater agency first, you'll commit to markets too small to matter.**

Second: greater commitment (Chapter 9). Only after creating something worth fighting for can you develop strategic stubbornness. Markets worth transforming take decades, not quarters. You'll learn how Steven Neuner's 20 years of 90-day reviews created compound momentum and how Sara Blakely persisted through seven years of rejection before her $1.2 billion exit. **Without greater commitment second, you'll abandon your revolution at first resistance.**

Third: greater courage (Chapter 10). Courage comes last because it requires both a worthy market AND proven commitment. You'll discover how Paul Abel lost everything three times—after he'd already committed to his mission—and rebuilt bigger each time, how Howard Schultz faced 242 rejections but persisted because his vision was worth the terror. **Without greater courage third, you'll never make the bets that matter.**

Get the sequence wrong, and you get:

- Courage without agency = brave stupidity

- Commitment without vision = persistent irrelevance
- Agency without guts = brilliant cowardice

Get it right, and you join the 5.4% who transform industries.

THE HIDDEN COST OF PLAYING SMALL WITH BIG FREEDOM

Every day you use autonomy for comfort instead of creating costs.

- Autonomous operators: 8–12x EBITDA
- Market creators: 15–30x EBITDA
- Industry transformers: up to 50x EBITDA
- On $5 million EBITDA: $100–$140 million left on the table

THE AFTERNOON THAT CHANGED COMMERCE FOREVER

Patrick Collison. John Collison. 2010. Seven lines of code. Patrick had complete freedom, having sold his first company—Auctomatic—for $5 million at the age of 19. He and his brother John could have retired, invested safely, and lived comfortably. Instead, together they wrote seven lines of code that would become Stripe.

Those seven lines weren't about need—they had money. They weren't about obligation—they had freedom. They were about Stage 4: using autonomy to architect what should exist. Online payments were broken, complex, and inaccessible to most developers. The Collisons simply decided to fix it.

Today Stripe carries a $129 billion valuation at the close of 2025, powering internet commerce for millions of businesses in over 100 countries. Built by two brothers who had nothing to prove and everything to give.

But here's the revelation: Every entrepreneur in Stage 4 has their "seven lines of code" moment—the moment they choose transformation over comfort. Patrick and John Collison didn't stumble into it. They chose it, deliberately and completely.

THE INTEGRATION THAT CHANGES EVERYTHING

Stage 4 only works when all three forces multiply each other:

Agency x Commitment x Courage = Exponential Impact

- Your agency creates markets worth decades of dedication.
- Your commitment sustains creation through years of resistance.
- Your courage enables bets that transform civilizations.

This is how:

- Collison built the payment infrastructure for the Internet age.
- Brian Chesky of Airbnb transformed how humanity experiences travel.
- Huang created the foundation for the AI revolution.
- Musk is systematically making humanity multiplanetary.

They didn't just achieve freedom. They used it to force evolution.

THE 18-MONTH COUNTDOWN

By 2027, these three forces will converge to redefine every industry:

- **AI commoditizing all operational advantages** (your efficiency becoming table stakes)
- **Gen Z redefining value itself** (your assumptions becoming obsolete)
- **$124 trillion wealth transfer** (funding transformation, not optimization)

Right now, while you're using freedom for comfort:

- A 26-year-old is architecting your industry's replacement.
- A competitor is creating the category that makes yours irrelevant.
- A transformation is beginning that will make your success meaningless.

You have 18 months to decide: Use your autonomy to defend yesterday or define tomorrow.

YOUR NEXT 72 HOURS OF TRANSFORMATION

By the time you finish Chapter 10, you'll have:

1. The agency blueprint: create markets that shouldn't exist but must

2. The commitment system: persist for decades when others pivot in quarters
3. The courage framework: transform terror into your strategic advantage
4. The integration formula: multiply all three forces exponentially
5. Proof: Realize that freedom without transformation is just expensive stagnation.

But more important, you'll have answered the question that's destroying your sleep: What will you do with your freedom that's worthy of what it cost to achieve?

THE CHOICE AT THIS PRECIPICE

Tomorrow morning, you'll wake to the same freedom, the same options, the same infinite possibilities.

But now you face the choice that separates the comfortable from the revolutionary: Will you be Blockbuster's CEO, helping it optimize for obsolescence? Or will you be Jensen Huang, betting everything on an invisible future?

Will you use your autonomy for leisure or for legacy?

Stage 4 isn't comfortable. Huang bled money for a decade. Collison dropped out of MIT. Every hotel chain mocked Chesky. But they all discovered something the 94.6% never will: **The most significant risk isn't betting your freedom on transformation. It's wasting it on comfort.**

Turn the page. Your transformation—and your industry's—awaits.

The machine runs without you. Now it's time to build the future that requires you.

CHAPTER 8

GREATER AGENCY—FROM REACTING TO CREATING MARKETS

While others optimize for today's game, you're designing tomorrow's playing field—forcing entire industries to adapt to your vision.

THE TUESDAY THAT CHANGED EVERYTHING

2:47 A.M. A different calculation this time.

You're not worried about operations—Chapter 7, Greater Autonomy, solved that. Your business runs without you. You could disappear for six months, and revenue would grow. The self-managing systems you built are bulletproof.

But here's what's keeping you awake: You've mastered someone else's game.

Every strategic move you make is a reaction. A competitor launches something; you respond. The market shifts; you adapt. Regulations change; you comply. You're incredibly good at playing defense, optimizing your position on a playing field designed by someone else, constrained by rules you didn't write.

You have freedom, but you lack power. You have autonomy, but you lack agency.

Here's the realization that terrifies the 5.4%: Mastery of the current game is a liability in a world of exponential disruption. The 18-month window is closing. While you're optimizing your present, someone is architecting your replacement.

The competitor you dismissed three years ago just raised $50 million to eliminate the constraint your entire industry accepts as a law of physics. They aren't trying to beat you; they are trying to make you irrelevant.

You have achieved Stage 3 liberation. Now you stand at the threshold of Stage 4: Exponential Impact.

The choice is stark: Will you use your autonomy to optimize the existing game? Or will you leverage your agency to design an entirely new one?

It's time to stop playing the game and start designing the playing field.

THE 5.4% INSIGHT: CATEGORY CREATION OVER COMPETITION

Our Greater Multipliers Study reveals who actually shapes markets:

- The 5.4% are market makers: 49.1% define new standards or paradigms, prompting entire industries to adjust.

- Other entrepreneurs are market takers: Only 16.0% set standards—the rest react to changes others create.

The data confirms the market reality: The 5.4% don't compete within categories—they create them.

This is the essence of greater agency: the power to define the rules of the game. It is achieved through a discipline called "category design."

THE 18-MONTH WINDOW (REVISITED): WHY AGENCY IS NO LONGER OPTIONAL

The convergence of AI, the massive wealth transfer, and the premium on category creation (introduced in Chapter 1) make greater agency mandatory.

AI is commoditizing execution at an unprecedented rate. Operational excellence is table stakes. In a world where execution is automated, vision becomes the only defensible moat.

The market rewards creators, not competitors.

- **Category competitors (the 94.6% trap):** 3–5x EBITDA
- **Category creators (the 5.4% zone):** 15–30x+ EBITDA

Agency isn't just about growth; it's about survival.

THE THREE LEVELS OF MARKET ENGAGEMENT

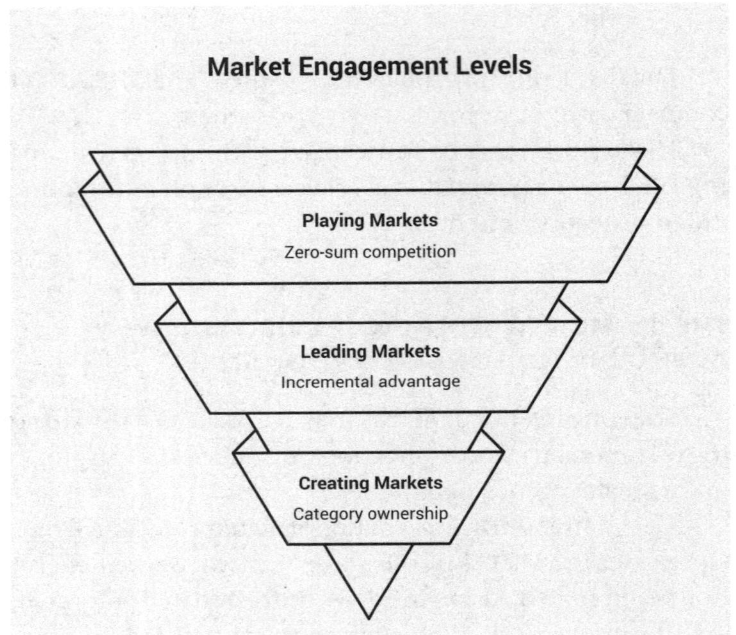

The 5.4% understand the distinction between the three levels of market engagement. Where are you playing?

Level 1: Playing Markets (the 94.6% Trap):

- **The mindset:** reactive, competitive, zero-sum competition
- **The strategy:** optimize existing models; compete on price and features
- **The outcome:** linear growth; vulnerability to disruption

Level 2: Leading Markets (the Optimization Zone):

- **The mindset:** proactive, innovative, best practices
- **The strategy:** improve existing models; differentiate through execution
- **The outcome:** incremental growth; temporary advantage

Level 3: Creating Markets (the 5.4% Zone):

- **The mindset:** architectural, revolutionary, positive-sum creation
- **The strategy:** design new categories; eliminate accepted constraints
- **The outcome:** exponential growth; competitive irrelevance

The shift from Level 2 to Level 3 requires a fundamental change in architecture, not just strategy.

MARK YOUNG: THE $100 MILLION DEAD SPACE REVOLUTION

Mark Young was already running Jekyll+Hyde Labs, an advertising powerhouse responsible for $10 billion in retail product sales, when a dinner conversation revealed a billion-dollar blind spot everyone else had missed.

The Problem Hiding in Plain Sight

A Kroger executive complained over dinner: "Those blood pressure screening stations are costing us millions annually.

They've become jungle gyms for kids while parents wait for prescriptions."

Every pharmacy had them—archaic health screening machines that occupied valuable floor space, generated no revenue, and created maintenance headaches. The industry accepted them as necessary evils.

Young saw something different: thousands of mini billboards sitting idle in America's highest-traffic health locations.

The Category Creation

Young didn't optimize the machines. He replaced them entirely with PharmaVision—sleek digital kiosks displaying targeted health content and ads for products already on pharmacy shelves.

The Architecture:

- Replace dead machines with revenue-generating media screens
- Show only health-enhancing product ads (no junk food)
- Mix educational content with commerce
- Partner with pharmaceutical companies for premium placement
- Turn competitors into clients by creating an entirely new advertising channel

The Exponential Impact:

- **Scale:** 2,000+ pharmacy locations in three years

- **Reach:** 3 million daily viewers
- **Revenue:** created multimillion-dollar media network from zero
- **Multiplier effect:** competing ad agencies now buying space from Young
- **Valuation shift:** from pharmacy equipment vendor to health-tech media company

Young didn't compete for existing ad dollars—he created an advertising channel that never existed. Former competitors now pay him to access the network he invented.

"We've created a multimillion-dollar television network in three years, where previously zero had existed," Young states. "Agencies are buying from my agency—my rivals have become my multipliers."

CARTER FROELICH: THE $2 BILLION INFRASTRUCTURE BREAKTHROUGH

While Mark Young focused on redefining physical space, Carter Froelich tackled a systemic constraint that paralyzes entire industries: infrastructure funding.

Carter's consulting firm financed roads, utilities, and parks for Texas developers. But every project hit the same crushing bottleneck that everyone accepted as unchangeable.

The 7-Year Problem Nobody Questioned

When developers build public infrastructure, they wait 3–7 years for government reimbursement through municipal utility districts. The industry's "solution"? Sell your reimbursement rights to private investors at a brutal 16% discount.

Every developer accepted this financial torture as the cost of doing business. Froelich saw it differently: Why should developers finance public infrastructure with their own capital for nearly a decade?

The Geographic Hack That Changed Everything

Froelich's breakthrough wasn't improving the system—it was bypassing it entirely. If Texas laws created the delays, why not use other states' bond systems?

His solution: Partner with out-of-state bond issuers to create federally tax-exempt bonds that institutional investors could buy immediately. He called it the Launch Bond.

The Transformation:

- **Wait time:** from 3–7 years to 2.5 months
- **Cost of capital:** 16% discount → 6% interest
- **First proof:** $36 million bond, reimbursed in 4 months (July 2023)
- **Industry adoption:** "Launch Bond" becomes required terminology

The Exponential Impact:

- **Scale:** $2 billion in bonds issued (2023–2025)
- **Clients:** Starwood Land, Johnson Development, Hillwood Communities
- **Business growth:** 4x revenue in 12 months at 80% margins
- **Category ownership:** Developers now say, "This project won't work without a Launch Bond."

Froelich didn't just solve a financial problem—he eliminated a decades-old constraint everyone thought was permanent. Now the entire industry uses his language and his system.

"We're part of the industry vernacular now," Froelich states. "Nobody wants to be the pioneer, but once somebody gets through that pass where the gold is, they're all suddenly buying Levi's and pickaxes."

Froelich didn't just create a better financial product; he architected a new system that eliminated a decades-old constraint. He compelled the entire industry to adopt his vision.

THE NEXT GENERATION OF MARKET CREATORS

While Young and Froelich transformed their industries through decades of experience, a new generation proves that market creation has no age requirement. They're not waiting for permission or expertise—they're creating categories before they turn 30.

THE $82 BILLION AIR MATTRESS REVOLUTION

Twenty-six-year-old Brian Chesky and his roommate Joe Gebbia couldn't make rent. It was 2007; a design conference had booked every hotel in San Francisco, and they had three air mattresses. That weekend constraint would birth a category worth tens of billions.

THE PROBLEM EVERYONE ACCEPTED

Hotels owned hospitality. They controlled supply, set prices, and defined what accommodation meant. Travelers had two choices: pay hotel rates or not travel. Chesky and Gebbia saw it differently: Why should hospitality require hotels at all?

THE CATEGORY CREATION JOURNEY

Phase 1: The Joke (2007–2008)

- Built a website called "Air Bed and Breakfast"
- First weekend: three guests, $240
- VCs rejected repeatedly: "No one will stay in a stranger's home"
- Hotels didn't even notice

Phase 2: The Platform (2009–2011)

- Built trust systems—reviews, verification, and insurance
- Expanded from air mattresses to entire homes
- Hotels started asking questions

Phase 3: The Category (2012–2015)

- Created "Belong Anywhere"—not just lodging but belonging
- Forced cities worldwide to write entirely new regulations
- Hotels scrambled to launch competitive responses

Phase 4: The New Reality (2016–Present)

- Every major hotel chain now has a home-sharing division
- Cities have Airbnb-specific laws
- "Alternative accommodations" is standard industry terminology

The Exponential Impact:

- **Scale:** 8+ million listings—more than all hotel chains combined
- **Reach:** 220+ countries, more than 2 billion guest arrivals
- **Market cap:** $82 billion at the close of 2025
- **Category dominance:** Forced Marriott, Hilton, and Hyatt into home-sharing

The Hotel Industry's Forced Evolution:

- 2008: "Nobody will use this."
- 2012: "It's not safe or regulated."
- 2016: "We need our own platform."
- 2025: "We're acquiring home-sharing companies."

Chesky and Gebbia's vision—that belonging matters more than branded bedding—permanently redefined travel. Their goal was never to build a better hotel. It was to create something hotels could never be: a way to belong anywhere.

They didn't compete with hotels. They rendered them obsolete for an entire category, forcing a $600 billion industry to adapt to their game.

PATRICK COLLISON AND JOHN COLLISON (STRIPE)

Two Irish brothers in their early 20s, with no prior experience in the payment industry, saw what everyone else accepted as unchangeable: accepting online payments was a monthslong nightmare.

THE PROBLEM EVERYONE ENDURED

Before Stripe, launching online payments meant:

- Months of bank negotiations
- Complex API integrations requiring specialized developers
- Separate accounts for each country
- Regulatory compliance maze
- 3–5.4% transaction fees, plus setup costs
- Weeks of testing before going live

PayPal existed but was clunky. Square focused on physical retail. Banks didn't understand the Internet. Every start-up lost momentum waiting for payment infrastructure.

THE SEVEN-LINE REVOLUTION

The Collisons asked a different question: What if accepting payments was as simple as copying and pasting code?

Their answer: Seven lines of code. Paste it into your website. You're now accepting payments globally.

The Transformation:

- **Setup time:** from months to minutes
- **Integration complexity:** from specialized teams to any developer
- **Geographic limitations:** from a single country to 47 countries instantly
- **Documentation:** from 500-page PDFs to interactive tutorials
- **Testing:** from weeks to immediate sandbox mode

The Exponential Impact:

- **Valuation:** ~$129 billion (based on secondary market activity, December 2025)
- **Scale:** powers 1.35 million active businesses, including Amazon, Google, and half the Fortune 100
- **Market share:** processes $1.4 trillion annually—more than the GDP of Australia
- **Category created:** developer-first payment infrastructure

- **GDP impact:** enabled thousands of companies that couldn't have existed without simple payments

The Forced Industry Evolution:

- **PayPal:** scrambled to rebuild its entire developer experience
- **Square:** shifted focus to compete for online payments
- **Banks:** created innovation labs and fintech partnerships
- **Amazon:** uses Stripe for parts of its own infrastructure
- **New reality:** every payment company now measuring itself against "Stripe-simple"

"We're not competing for payment share," Patrick Collison states. "We're increasing the GDP of the Internet."

The profound twist: Stripe Connect lets anyone become a payment platform using Stripe's infrastructure. Competitors don't fight Stripe—they build on it, making Stripe stronger with every new platform they introduce.

DANIEL EK (SPOTIFY): THE $120 BILLION PIRACY SOLUTION

Daniel Ek was 22, had never worked inside the music industry, and proposed something it called suicide: Give away all music for free. Today, Spotify is worth $120 billion and saved the recording industry.

The Problem Destroying Music

In 2006, the music industry was dying:

- CD sales were collapsing 20% annually
- Napster and LimeWire had trained a generation that music was free
- iTunes charged $0.99 per song — but why pay when piracy was easier?
- Record labels were suing their own customers (30,000+ lawsuits.)
- Artists were making pennies while lawyers got rich.

The industry's solution? More lawsuits, higher prices, more restrictions.

THE PIRATE'S INSIGHT

Ek had been a pirate himself. He knew why people stole music: It wasn't about money — it was about friction. Piracy was easier than purchasing. His insight: What if you could access all the world's music, instantly, legally, for the price of a single CD per month?

The Solution:

- Free tier with ads (converting pirates to users)
- Paid tier for $9.99/month (less than the cost of one CD)
- Instant access to 100 million songs

- Playlists that replaced the radio
- Algorithm that knew your taste better than you did

The Exponential Impact:

- **Scale:** 751 million users, 290 million paid subscribers (Q4 2025)
- **Market cap:** $120 billion at the close of 2025
- **Industry:** Streaming now generates ~84% of music industry revenue
- **Artist payments:** $40+ billion paid to rights holders since launch
- **Category created:** Music streaming is now how humanity consumes music

The Forced Industry Evolution:

- **Record labels:** From suing Spotify to owning equity in it
- **Apple:** Forced to launch Apple Music — their iTunes model destroyed
- **Amazon/Google/YouTube:** Had to create competing streaming services
- **Radio:** Effectively replaced by streaming playlists
- **Music ownership:** Became obsolete — consumers moved from owning to accessing

Ek's insight — that access beats ownership — permanently redefined how the world hears music. He didn't save the music industry on its terms. He forced it to abandon its entire business model for his. The proof: vinyl outsold CDs for the fifth consecutive year in 2025 — physical music became nostalgia while streaming became a utility.

THE COMMON ARCHITECTURE

1. **They identified an accepted constraint** that everyone else ignored.
2. **They envisioned a new reality** where that constraint was eliminated.
3. **They named the new category,** defining the new paradigm.
4. **They architected the ecosystem**, aligning stakeholders around the new reality.

THE MYTHS OF AGENCY (AND HOW TO DISMANTLE THEM)

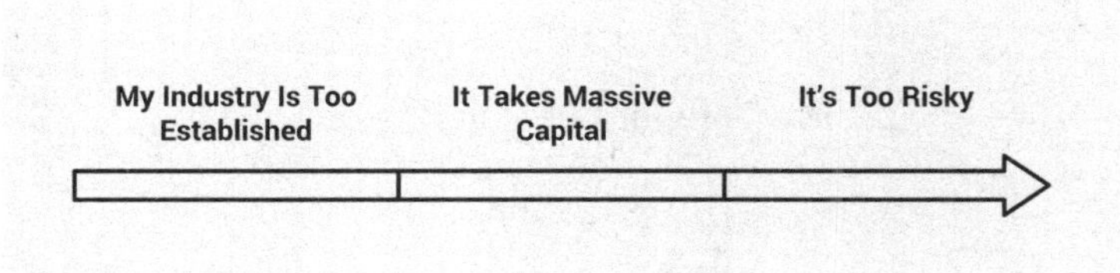

Three myths keep the 94.6% trapped in reactive optimization.

Myth 1: My Industry Is Too Established. (It Can't Be Changed.)

Reality: Every industry is established until someone changes it. Banking (Stripe), hospitality (Airbnb), music

(Spotify), and infrastructure funding (Launch Bond)—all were considered immutable until they weren't. The more established the industry, the greater the opportunity for transformation.

Myth 2: Category Creation Requires Massive Capital. (I Don't Have the Resources.)

Reality: Category creation requires vision, not just capital. Airbnb started with air mattresses. Stripe started with seven lines of code. PharmaVision started with one pharmacy. Vision precedes resources.

Myth 3: It's Too Risky. (I Could Lose Everything.)

Reality: The most significant risk is optimizing an obsolete model. Playing the existing game guarantees eventual irrelevance. Creating the new game is the only path to sustainable success.

THE CATEGORY DESIGN BLUEPRINT: HOW TO CREATE YOUR MARKET

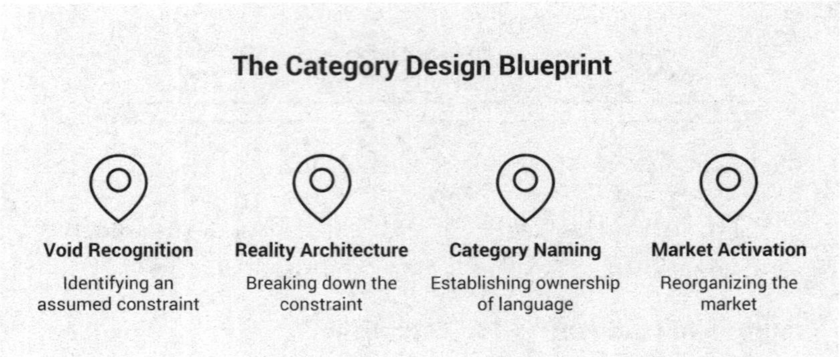

The Category Design Blueprint

Void Recognition
Identifying an assumed constraint

Reality Architecture
Breaking down the constraint

Category Naming
Establishing ownership of language

Market Activation
Reorganizing the market

The 5.4% don't wait for markets to emerge; they design them. Here is the four-phase blueprint for achieving greater agency.

Phase 1: Void Recognition (Identify the Constraint)

Identify the unspoken rules and accepted frictions in your industry. What is the constraint that everyone assumes is unchangeable?

- *Ask:* What problem are we solving that shouldn't exist?
- *Ask:* What friction are we optimizing that we should eliminate?

Phase 2: Reality Architecture (Envision the New Paradigm)

Imagine a future where this constraint is eliminated. What new behavior, business model, or opportunity becomes possible?

- *Define* the new reality without the constraint.
- *Design* the architecture (technology, business model, ecosystem) that enables this new reality.

Phase 3: Category Naming (Own the Language)

To own a category, you must name it. Create a memorable, proprietary name for this new reality. This is how you shift the industry vernacular.

- *Create* the proprietary name (e.g., Launch Bond, PharmaVision).
- *Articulate* the manifesto that defines the new category and makes the old way feel obsolete.

Phase 4: Market Activation (Launch the Revolution)

Introduce the new category to the market. Evangelize the new reality. Force the industry to adapt to your vision.

- *Evangelize* the problem, not the product.
- *Educate* the market on the new paradigm.
- *Mobilize* the ecosystem around the new category.

THE CHOICE: DEFINER OR DEFINED?

You have reached the first step of Stage 4: Exponential Impact. You understand the power of shifting from reacting to markets to creating them.

The choice is now yours: Will you continue to optimize for today's game, reacting to the moves of others, or will you strive to anticipate and outmaneuver them? Or will you design tomorrow's playing field, forcing entire industries to adapt to your vision?

By 2027, every market will be redefined. The only question is: Will you be the definer or the defined?

THE BRIDGE TO GREATER COMMITMENT

Greater agency empowers you to create new categories. But creation without commitment is just experimentation.

In Chapter 9, Greater Commitment, you will discover the power of strategic stubbornness—the discipline of maintaining vision immutability while ensuring tactical flexibility. You will learn how to navigate the inevitable resistance, setbacks, and distractions that accompany revolutionary change.

It's time to move from creation to establishment.

ACTIVATE YOUR TECHNOLOGY MULTIPLIER

THE BRIDGE: FROM REACTING TO ARCHITECTING

You have achieved greater autonomy. Your business runs without you. You have the freedom that 94.6% only dream of. Now comes the critical choice of Stage 4: What will you do with that freedom?

The 94.6% use their autonomy to optimize the existing game. They react more quickly, adapt more effectively, and compete more fiercely within the rules defined by others. They become wealthy irrelevancies, defending a playing field designed by someone else, vulnerable to the 18-month disruption window that is already closing.

The 5.4%, like Young, Froelich, Chesky, Collison, and Ek, use their autonomy as a launching pad for revolution. They understand that the most significant opportunities lie not in capturing market share but in creating entirely new categories where competition is irrelevant. They don't react to the future; they architect it, forcing entire industries to adapt to their vision.

It's time to stop playing the game and start designing the playing field.

THE MULTIPLIER ACTIVATION: THE CATEGORY DESIGN CHALLENGE

This exercise is designed to identify the market that *should* exist but doesn't and to position you as its architect. This is the blueprint for moving from competitive advantage to competitive irrelevance.

Step 1: Identify the Accepted Constraint (the Void)

Every industry operates with unspoken rules and accepted frictions that everyone assumes are unchangeable laws of physics. Identify the most significant constraint in your industry.

- *The "unchangeable" industry constraint:*

  ____

  ____

- *Examples: Carter Froelich and the 3–7 year wait for infrastructure reimbursement; Patrick Collison and the complexity of accepting payments online.*

Step 2: The Elimination (the New Reality)

Imagine a future where this constraint is eliminated, not just optimized. What new behavior, business model, or opportunity becomes possible?

- *The future reality without this constraint:*

  ____

  ____

- *Examples: Mark Young—dead pharmacy space becomes a vibrant health education network; Brian Chesky—anyone can turn their home into a hospitality experience.*

Step 3: Name the Category (the Ownership)

To own a category, you must name it. Create a memorable, proprietary name for this new reality. This is how you shift the industry vernacular.

- *My new category name:*

  ____

- *Examples: "Launch Bond," "PharmaVision," "Alternative Accommodations"*

Step 4: The Manifesto (the Declaration)

Write a single sentence that defines your new category and makes the old way feel obsolete.

- *My category manifesto:*

  ____

  ____

  ____

- *Examples: Chesky: "Belong Anywhere"; Ek: "All the world's music, instantly accessible."*

THE SCORECARD: MEASURE YOUR AGENCY

Quantify your current market creation readiness. Score yourself from 1 (reactive) to 12 (revolutionary) in each category:

Category	Description	Now (1–12)	12-Month Target
Void Recognition	I see opportunities others call impossible.	___	___
Standard Setting	I define what success means in my industry.	___	___
Category Creation	I've built markets that didn't exist.	___	___
Competitive Irrelevance	Competitors become collaborators in my paradigm.	___	___
Force Multiplication	Others adapt to my frameworks.	___	___
Industry Architecture	I design infrastructure that others depend on.	___	___
TOTAL SCORE:		___/ 72	

Score Interpretation:

- **6–30:** Playing markets (reactive; the 94.6% trap)
- **31–50:** Leading markets (proactive; optimization focus)
- **51–72:** Creating markets (revolutionary; the 5.4% zone)

THE DASHBOARD INTEGRATION: CREATE YOUR MARKET

Your Category Design Challenge and Scorecard are the first steps toward architecting your industry's future. Don't just imagine the future—quantify your readiness to build it.

Scan the QR code below or go to TheGreaterGame Dashboard.com and input your Greater Agency score.

Here's how the platform supports your market creation strategy:

1. **The "Category King" Benchmark:** How does your agency score compare to the entrepreneurs who define rather than compete in markets? The Entrepreneurial Pulse research identifies that 49.1% of the 5.4% set new standards or paradigms that force entire industries to adapt.

2. **The Command Center View:** Your agency score is the first metric in Stage 4: Exponential Impact. Track how it elevates your overall GMI (greater multipliers index) and impacts the 15–30x valuation multiples associated with market architects.
3. **Your Recommended Actions:** Based on your agency architecture, the platform surfaces personalized pathways:
    - **VFO Second Opinion**—If your category creation requires capital deployment, acquisition strategy, or complex deal structures, this pathway provides the wealth architecture for bold market moves.
    - **Strategic Coach Acceleration**—If you're ready to create markets but lack the operational frameworks to execute, this pathway provides the systems to move from vision to industry transformation.

Every market will be redefined. The only question is: Will you be the definer or the defined? Activate your dashboard and start architecting the future now.

CHAPTER 9

GREATER COMMITMENT—THE COMPOUND EFFECT OF STRATEGIC STUBBORNNESS

While others pivot at every obstacle, you persist strategically—turning setbacks into jet fuel for your 25-year vision.

THE TUESDAY THAT ALMOST DESTROYED EVERYTHING

You're not worried about market creation—Chapter 8, Greater Agency, solved that. You've defined a new category. You've compelled competitors to adhere to your standards. The industry press calls you a visionary.

But here's what's keeping you awake—and what every market creator discovers: The real test isn't creation; it's conviction. Building the market takes courage. Establishing it takes commitment.

Three board members just called an emergency meeting. Your biggest investor is nervous. Your team is questioning the vision. The market isn't adopting as quickly as projected.

Everyone wants you to pivot. To be "realistic." To pursue the safer path.

Last week, a well-meaning advisor said, "Maybe you're being too stubborn. The market is telling you something."

That's when you felt it—the gravitational pull back to the 94.6%. The seductive whisper that says, "Just optimize what works. Stop trying to change the world."

Your daughter asked at dinner, "Why do you keep pushing when everyone says to stop?"

You couldn't answer. The truth is, you're not sure whether you're being strategically persistent or stubbornly expensive.

You've created a new market. Now comes the real test: Do you commit to see it through?

THE UNWAVERING COMMITMENT GAP

As you read this, our research indicates that 79.7% of entrepreneurs lack consistent commitment to their long-term vision. The vast majority allow immediate pressures to divert their course.

This isn't because their vision was wrong. It's because they couldn't distinguish strategic persistence from expensive stubbornness.

Our Greater Multipliers Study of 1,016 entrepreneurs reveals the brutal truth about commitment:

Among all entrepreneurs surveyed:

- Only 20.3% maintain unwavering commitment, where every decision stems from a deeply ingrained long-term perspective.

- Just 18.5% show unwavering focus, using setbacks as fuel for more significant breakthroughs.
- A mere 33.7% ensure daily activities reflect their long-term vision and measure alignment.

But among $50+ million entrepreneurs, the pattern shifts dramatically:

- 28.1% demonstrate unwavering commitment to their long-term vision.
- 29.2% actively use setbacks as stepping-stones to exponential breakthroughs.
- 41.6% maintain rigorous discipline, executing large-scale initiatives that reinforce exponential goals.

The data are undeniable: The wealthiest entrepreneurs don't just persist—they persist strategically, with 45.6% adapting their strategies while remaining committed to the end goal.

This isn't about a specific timeline. It's about a fundamental difference in approach. The 5.4% build systems to maintain vision clarity, while others drift toward whatever seems urgent today.

STEVEN NEUNER: 20 YEARS OF STAYING ON TARGET

Steven Neuner discovered the power of strategic commitment not in a boardroom but in a moment of brutal clarity about his own life.

THE 25-YEAR VISION

Twenty years ago, at 31, Neuner was drowning. Deep in debt. Running a struggling insurance agency in Dallas. New father. Zero clarity about the future.

"I knew what I wanted freedom from," he recalls. "But I couldn't have told you what I wanted freedom to go and do."

His business coach asked him to write down his ideal life decades into the future. For the first time, Neuner permitted himself to imagine a life of purpose, not just profit. He wrote a vision centered on faith, marriage, financial independence, restored family relationships, and building something that mattered.

Then came the discipline that separates the 94.6% from the 5.4%: He has revisited and revised that vision every 90 days for the past 20 years.

The 90-day question isn't "Am I on track?" It's "Is my track still taking me where I want to go?" That is the difference between motion and progress.

THE STRATEGIC "NO" SYSTEM

"Ideas show up all the time," Neuner says. "But if they don't align with the bigger future I've already committed to, they don't make the cut."

This isn't rigidity—it's strategic filtering. Every opportunity gets measured against the same questions:

- Does it fit the lifetime vision?
- Does it move the mission forward?
- Does it multiply freedom and growth—not just for himself but also for others?

The 94.6% chase every promising opportunity. Neuner's commitment permitted him to say no to good so he could say yes to great.

THE COMPOUND ACCELERATION

By staying committed to empowering entrepreneurs—a drive instilled in him by watching a relative's small business develop during his childhood—Neuner built his insurance agency into a $25 million company.

But here's where strategic commitment differs from blind persistence: In 2019, he exited.

"It was difficult walking away from a business I built with people I love, but it was the next 'right' step to remain faithful to the vision."

The exit wasn't abandonment—it was evolution. He saw it as "graduate school, and ultimately a graduation."

THE SECOND ACT MULTIPLICATION

In 2020, Neuner co-founded Superpowers—connecting entrepreneurs with elite executive assistants (EA's) trained in "flipped delegation," where the EA leads proactively.

The results of 20 years of commitment clarity were:

- 100% year-over-year growth
- $4 million annual recurring revenue
- 100% referral-based (zero marketing spend)
- Debt-free, investor-free operations

"What took me 15 years to build the first time, we did in three at Superpowers," says Neuner. "That's what commitment and clarity do."

THE LIFE INTEGRATION PROOF

Strategic commitment didn't just build businesses—it built a life. Neuner's strategy means he can enjoy the following perks:

- 150+ free days annually
- Weekly date nights for nearly two decades
- Road tripped to nearly every U.S. state with his kids
- A new venture running BarnHill Vineyards—a family venue teaching entrepreneurial values

"That's why I wake up excited to keep building, because staying on purpose still stretches me," he says. "It's not about what's most exciting in the moment but what's still aligned the next morning. That's what staying on purpose looks like."

The lesson: Neuner didn't just commit to a business. He committed to a vision that transcended any single venture. That's strategic stubbornness.

JERRY BROWDER: THE RELENTLESS PURSUIT OF A MISSION

While Neuner committed to a life vision, Jerry Browder demonstrates what happens when you commit to a mission for over four decades.

THE SINGULAR FOCUS

For more than 40 years, Browder has stayed relentlessly committed to one vision: advocating for the vulnerable when they cannot advocate for themselves.

This wasn't a convenient mission. In 1999, after being fired twice from the same corporation where he'd worked for 12 years, Browder could have chosen any path.

"The more I worked for others, the more I saw that I'm an entrepreneur down to my toes," he says.

But instead of chasing the hottest opportunity, he chose health care—specifically mental health crisis management. Not because it was easy but because it mattered.

"It's the largest industry in the U.S., and the largest diagnostic category of spending within health care is mental illness and addiction," he explains. "The health care industry is the perfect place to put your attention."

THE 20-YEAR PREPARATION

From 1999 to 2020, Browder gradually grew Signet Health to approximately $10 million in annual revenue. The 94.6% would call this modest success. Browder saw it as preparation.

"I didn't have the money to buy these firms, but I still went ahead and spent years making overtures to them," he says. "It was pure persistence."

Think about that: years pursuing acquisitions he couldn't afford. He wasn't hoping for luck; he was building toward inevitability.

THE PERSISTENCE PAYOFF

After pursuing nearly 30 acquisitions and achieving only two, Browder landed the deal that validated two decades of commitment.

- **Target:** his largest competitor
- **Size:** five times larger than Signet
- **Owner:** $16 billion publicly traded company
- **Financing:** 100% seller and third-party financing
- **Result:** went from 60 to 700+ employees overnight

Today, Signet Health is the largest provider of inpatient contract management services to hospitals nationwide. Its valuation has increased 16x over the past five years.

THE MISSION MULTIPLICATION

But Browder's commitment isn't to size—it's to mission. His vision for the next decade: "Depending on the location, between 30% and 70% of our patients would take their own lives if they had the opportunity. I have a belief that in the next 10 years, we will potentially be able to advocate at some level for substantially every mentally ill patient in America."

The 94.6% would call this unrealistic. Browder calls it inevitable.

"It's a big vision and a big mission, but just watch us—we're going to do it."

The lesson: Forty years of commitment to a singular mission created the credibility, capability, and conviction to acquire a competitor 5x his size with zero cash down. That's what strategic stubbornness compounds into.

SARA BLAKELY: WHEN NEAR-TOTAL REJECTION BECOMES $1.2 BILLION

While Neuner and Browder show commitment at the enterprise level, Sara Blakely demonstrates what happens when strategic stubbornness redefines an entire industry.

THE TWO-YEAR NO

For nearly two years, Blakely heard no from every manufacturer, retailer, and investor she approached. But she discovered something more powerful than market validation: strategic stubbornness based on customer truth, not industry opinion.

Manufacturers said no because they'd never done it. Retailers said no because the category didn't exist. But customers—when she showed them prototypes, their eyes lit up.

THE COMMITMENT ARCHITECTURE

Blakely built a systematic approach to persistence:

- **Every no becomes data:** She tracked rejection patterns to sharpen her pitch
- **Pivot tactics, not vision:** The product never changed; the presentation evolved constantly
- **Constraints as catalysts:** No marketing budget led to mailing Oprah a prototype—worth more than $10 million when Oprah named Spanx a Favorite Thing in 2000

The Quantified Result:

- **Investment:** $5,000 in personal savings
- **Time to first yes:** Approximately two years
- **Valuation at sale:** $1.2 billion (Blackstone, 2021)
- **Category dominance:** No competitor displaced Spanx as leader during 21 years of ownership

Blakely's commitment wasn't to proving the industry wrong. It was to the women who needed a solution it had never bothered to create.

THE AI AMPLIFICATION OF COMMITMENT

While 94.6% use AI for efficiency, the 5.4% use it for commitment architecture. Whether you use Scorecards, OKRs, or 90-Day Rocks, AI can now track your alignment and highlight drift before it becomes dangerous.

Neuner's vision gets reviewed by AI pattern recognition every quarter. Browder's acquisition targets are identified through AI market analysis. Your strategic stubbornness can now be systematically supported by technology that never forgets your *why*.

AI doesn't replace your commitment—it amplifies it:

- Track vision alignment across all decisions.
- Identify patterns in setbacks that lead to breakthroughs.
- Automate the "no" to opportunities that don't align.
- Create early warning systems for commitment drift.

The technology handles the tracking while you handle the transformation.

THE STRATEGIC STUBBORNNESS SYSTEM

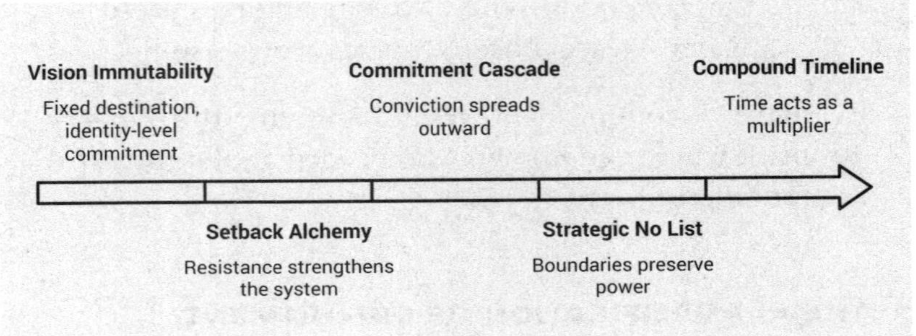

The 5.4% don't just persist—they architect strategic stubbornness through five transformative principles.

Principle 1: Vision Immutability, Tactical Flexibility

- **94.6% approach:** either rigid on everything or flexible on everything
- **5.4% architecture:** fixed on destination, fluid on path

Your 25-year vision: carved in stone
Your 90-day tactics: written in sand
Your annual strategy: firm but reversible

- **Neuner's application:** The life vision never changed; businesses evolved to serve it.
- **Browder's discipline:** The mission stayed constant; the acquisition strategy adapted.

- **Blakely's framework:** The product vision was fixed; presentation was constantly refined.

Principle 2: Setback Alchemy

- **94.6% response:** Setbacks are signals to stop.
- **5.4% system:** Setbacks are data for acceleration.

The Alchemy Framework:

1. Document the setback precisely.
2. Extract three learnings within 48 hours.
3. Implement one improvement within seven days.
4. Share the learning with your team.
5. Track how this setback strengthened your position.

- **Neuner's example:** A software venture failure became "tuition for a vital lesson."
- **Browder's persistence:** 28 failed acquisitions taught him exactly how to land the 29th.

Principle 3: The Commitment Cascade

Strategic stubbornness multiplies through layers:

- **Personal commitment:** You embody the vision daily.
- **Team commitment:** Your conviction becomes contagious.
- **Customer commitment:** They become evangelists.
- **Market commitment:** The industry accepts your standard.
- **Legacy commitment:** The vision outlasts you.

Neuner's family runs the vineyard together. Browder's children joined Signet. Blakely's customers became her sales force.

Principle 4: The Strategic "No" List

What you won't do defines you more than what you will do. Document your strategic "No" list:

- Opportunities that dilute focus
- Partnerships that compromise values
- Shortcuts that undermine quality
- Pivots that abandon vision
- Voices that erode conviction
- **Neuner's filter:** "If they don't align with the bigger future I've already committed to, they don't make the cut."
- **Browder's boundary:** No ventures outside health care, regardless of returns.

Principle 5: The Compound Timeline

- **94.6% timeline:** quarterly results, annual plans
- **5.4% timeline:** decades of development

Neuner: 20 years of 90-day reviews
Browder: 40+ years in health care
Blakely: 21 years of sole ownership

Each year of commitment makes the next year more powerful. Time becomes your ally, not your enemy.

THE GREATER COMMITMENT FRAMEWORK

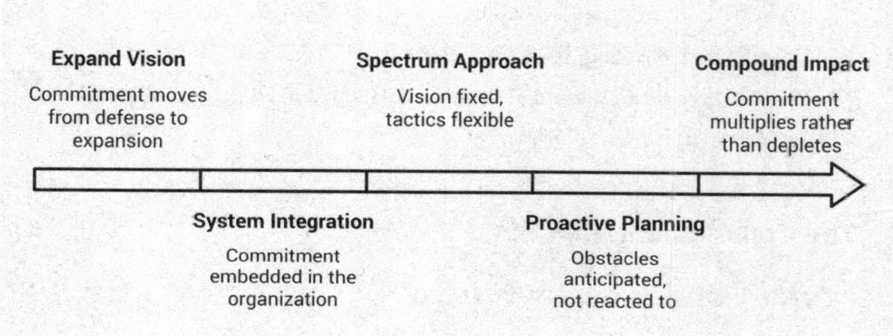

Transform scattered persistence into systematic advancement through five multiplying shifts.

Shift 1: From Defending to Expanding

Stop protecting what you've built. Start expanding what's possible.

- Defensive commitment: maintaining position
- Expansive commitment: growing through challenges

Neuner sold his first company to build a bigger one. Browder acquired competitors to expand the mission's reach.

Shift 2: From Solo to System

Your commitment must become organizational DNA.

- Individual persistence: exhausting
- Systematic persistence: energizing

Browder's team includes his children. Neuner's vision shapes every hire.

Shift 3: From Binary to Spectrum

Not "pivot or persist," but "what should evolve while the vision remains?"

The Commitment Spectrum:

- Core Vision: 100% fixed
- Strategic Approach: 80% stable
- Tactical Execution: 60% stable
- Daily Operations: 40% stable
- Experimental Initiatives: 20% stable

Shift 4: From Reactive to Proactive

Don't wait for obstacles—anticipate and prepare for them.

The Obstacle Anticipation Protocol:

1. List 10 likely obstacles to your vision.
2. Design responses before they occur.
3. Build capabilities that make obstacles irrelevant.
4. Create early warning systems.
5. Turn defense into offense.

Browder spent years preparing for acquisitions he couldn't yet afford.

Shift 5: From Exhausting to Compound

Make commitment compound rather than deplete.

The Compound Formula: Clarity x Consistency x Time = Exponential Impact

Neuner says, "What took me 15 years to build the first time, we did in three at Superpowers."

YOUR COMMITMENT ARCHITECTURE FRAMEWORK

Transform strategic stubbornness from concept to system through three interconnected pillars that you build at your own pace.

Pillar 1: Clarify Your Immutables

Start here, regardless of where you are in your journey:

- Write your 25-year vision in one sentence.
- List 10 things you'll never compromise.
- Document your strategic "no" list.
- Share your vision with 100 people.
- Track who resonates versus who resists.

Follow Neuner's model: Review and refine every 90 days, no matter how long you've been at it.

Pillar 2: Build Your Persistence Protocol

Layer these systems as you're ready:

- Design your setback alchemy system.
- Create obstacle anticipation maps.
- Establish daily commitment rituals.

- Build accountability structures.
- Document early wins and lessons.

Apply Browder's approach: Track every attempt, learn from every no—whether it's your first or your fiftieth.

Pillar 3: Scale Your Stubbornness

Expand your commitment through your ecosystem:

- Embed commitment in team culture.
- Create customer commitment programs.
- Build market education systems.
- Establish measurement frameworks.
- Celebrate strategic persistence publicly.

Use Blakely's method: Turn customers into evangelists at whatever stage you've reached.

These pillars aren't sequential—they're symbiotic. You might start by clarifying your team culture before defining your vision. You may need to establish persistence protocols as you scale. The key is consistent application, not perfect timing.

THE HIDDEN COST OF FLEXIBILITY

Every abandoned vision costs more than money.

Valuation Impact:

- Persistent founders: 12–15x EBITDA multiples
- Pivoting founders: 3–5x EBITDA multiples
- **The commitment premium: more than $50 million at exit**

Browder's 16x valuation increase. Blakely's $1.2 billion exit. These aren't accidents—they're the compound effect of strategic stubbornness.

The critical truth: You'll never know how close you were if you bail right before the compounding kicks in. The 94.6% quit three feet from gold. The 5.4% dig until they strike it.

Team Impact:

- A-players follow committed leaders.
- B-players follow wherever the wind blows.
- Your commitment level determines your talent level.

Neuner attracts 100% referrals. Browder's team includes family. Commitment attracts commitment.

Life Impact:

- Neuner: 150+ free days, deep family connection, multiple ventures
- Browder: a legacy of advocating for the vulnerable
- Blakely: empowering women globally

Strategic stubbornness doesn't just build wealth—it creates a life that matters.

THE CHOICE: PIVOT OR PERSIST?

That emergency board meeting tomorrow? That nervous investor? That exhausted team?

They're not obstacles. They are opportunities to prove your commitment.

Will you choose the safety of the pivot, or the power of persistence?

Steven Neuner chose persistence for 20 years. Jerry Browder chose it for 40. Sara Blakely chose it through seven years of rejection.

They didn't just build businesses. They built legacies.

Now it's your turn. Commit. Persist. Compound.

THE BRIDGE: FROM REACTIVE PIVOTING TO STRATEGIC PERSISTENCE

You have recognized the gravitational pull of the 94.6%—the constant pressure to pivot, to be "realistic," and to abandon your long-term vision for short-term safety. You've felt the confusion between expensive stubbornness and strategic persistence.

The 94.6% confuse flexibility with a lack of conviction. They pivot at the first sign of resistance, driven by immediate pressures and external validation. They chase excitement in the moment rather than alignment with the future. This path leads to diluted impact, lower valuations (3–5x), and a legacy of abandoned possibilities.

The 5.4%, like Steven Neuner, Jerry Browder, and Sara Blakely, understand the compound effect of strategic stubbornness. They don't just persist; they persist strategically. They maintain an unwavering commitment to their 25-year vision (vision immutability) while remaining tactically flexible. They utilize systems like the 90-day review and setback alchemy to transform obstacles into fuel for growth and development. This is the path to exponential impact and 15x+ valuations.

It's time to stop reacting to the present and start compounding your future.

THE MULTIPLIER ACTIVATION: THE STRATEGIC STUBBORNNESS MATRIX

This exercise is designed to help you distinguish between your immutable vision and your flexible tactics. It will enable you to navigate pressure and adapt your approach without abandoning your core commitment.

Step 1: Define the Immutable Vision (the 25-Year Commitment)

Restate the core vision you are strategically stubborn about—the destination that will not change, regardless of the path.

- My immutable vision: ____________________

  ____

  ____

- *Example: Jerry Browder: Advocating for substantially every mentally ill patient in America.*

Step 2: Identify the Current Pressure (the Temptation to Pivot)

Name the specific obstacle, market feedback, or internal doubt currently pressuring you to abandon or significantly alter this vision.

- The current pressure to pivot: ______________

  ____

  ____

- *Examples: Market adoption slower than projected; key investor demanding a shift to a safer market.*

Step 3: Apply Setback Alchemy (Extract the Fuel)

Strategic persistence requires transforming setbacks into data. Identify the learning or capability this pressure forces you to develop.

- The learning/capability this forces me to develop:

  ____

  ____

  ____

  ____

- *Examples: Develop a more effective market education strategy; build stronger investor communication frameworks.*

Step 4: Design the Tactical Adaptation (the Flexible Move)

Define the specific tactical change you will make this quarter to address the pressure (Step 2) and leverage the learning (Step 3), while remaining 100% committed to the immutable vision (Step 1).

- *My tactical adaptation (flexible tactic, fixed vision):*

  ____

  ____

  ____

- *Example: Sara Blakely—the product vision never changed; the presentation evolved constantly.*

The Scorecard: Measure Your Commitment

Quantify your current level of strategic stubbornness. Score yourself from 1 (reactive pivoting) to 12 (strategic persistence) in each category.

Category	Description	Now (1–12)	12-Month Target
Vision Immutability	My 25-year vision remains fixed despite external pressure.	___	___
Tactical Flexibility	I adapt methods and strategies without abandoning my core vision.	___	___
Strategic No System	I have a clear filter for evaluating opportunities against my long-term vision.	___	___
Setback Alchemy	I systematically transform obstacles and rejections into advantages and fuel.	___	___
90-Day Rhythm	I maintain a regular 90-day rhythm of vision review and refinement.	___	___
Compound Timeline	I focus on decades of compounding, not quarterly wins.	___	___
TOTAL SCORE:		___ / 72	

Score Interpretation:

- **6–30:** Reactive pivoting (the 94.6% trap; high commitment drift)

- **31–50:** Building persistence (developing systems for commitment)
- **51–72:** Strategic stubbornness (the 5.4% zone; compounding impact)

THE DASHBOARD INTEGRATION: COMPOUND YOUR COMMITMENT

Your Strategic Stubbornness Matrix and Scorecard provide the critical data to move from reactive pivoting to systematic persistence. Don't let your vision drift—anchor it.

Scan the QR code below or go to TheGreaterGameDashboard.com and input your Greater Commitment score.

Here's how the platform supports your strategic stubbornness:

1. **The Commitment Benchmark:** Compare your score against the 28.1% of $50+ million entrepreneurs who maintain unwavering commitment—where every decision stems from their 25-year vision—versus the 79.7% who allow short-term pressures to divert them, as tracked by the Entrepreneurial Pulse.
2. **The Command Center View:** Your commitment score is a critical metric in Stage 4 (Exponential Impact). Track how strategic stubbornness elevates your overall GMI

(greater multipliers index) and compounds your progress across all other multipliers.

3. **Your Recommended Actions:** Based on your commitment architecture, the platform surfaces personalized pathways:
   - **VFO Second Opinion**—If commitment drift stems from financial distractions or wealth complexity pulling focus from your vision, this pathway eliminates the noise.
   - **Strategic Coach Acceleration**—If you need systematic frameworks to maintain strategic stubbornness while staying tactically flexible, this pathway provides the 90-day rhythms that compound over decades.

The 5.4% don't pivot under pressure—they persist with precision. Activate your dashboard and compound your commitment now.

CHAPTER 10

GREATER COURAGE—YOUR FEAR IS YOUR COMPASS

While others run from fear, you run toward it—transforming terror into the fuel that powers your 25-year vision.

THE CALL THAT CHANGES EVERYTHING

2:47 A.M. But you're not in bed this time.

You're in your office, staring at the offer letter that arrived yesterday. A strategic buyer wants to acquire your company for 15x EBITDA—three times what you expected. The number is life-changing: $180 million.

But here's what's keeping you awake: You're terrified to say yes. And you're frightened to say no.

Say yes, and you abandon the vision you've committed to for a decade. Say no, and you might be throwing away generational wealth. The safe move is obvious—take the money, eliminate the risk, secure the future.

Your spouse found you here an hour ago. "What are you afraid of?" they asked.

That's when you realized the truth that's destroying you: You're not afraid of failing. You're terrified of playing small.

The acquisition isn't just money—it's an escape hatch from the bigger game you know you should be playing. It's permission to stop before you've truly started. It's the 94.6% whispering, "You've done enough. Take the win. Don't risk it."

Your greater commitment (Chapter 9) has kept you strategically stubborn for years. You've persisted when others pivoted. You've built the market-creating agency that makes this acquisition possible.

But commitment without courage is just determination without daring. And right now, at 2:47 A.M., you're face-to-face with the question that separates the 5.4% from everyone else:

Will you choose the comfort of the exit, or the courage of your calling?

THE COURAGE CRISIS NOBODY ADMITS

Our Greater Multipliers Study reveals a hidden crisis.

Among 1,016 entrepreneurs surveyed:

- Only **22.1%** embrace significant risks as essential to transformative success.
- Just **16.1%** jump on big ideas immediately, adjusting as needed.
- A mere **25.9%** view failure as a stepping-stone to exponential breakthroughs.

But among $50+ million entrepreneurs, the pattern reverses:

- **39.3%** actively treat failure as fuel for their most significant breakthroughs.
- **33.7%** actively seek disruptive, unexplored opportunities.
- **47.2%** act decisively once they see a clear path, trusting their judgment.

The revelation that changes everything: The 5.4% aren't fearless. They're fear seeking.

They've discovered what neuroscience now proves: The same neural pathways that process fear also process excitement. The physiological response is nearly identical. The only difference is your interpretation of the sensation.

Consider this striking contrast: While **24.6%** of all entrepreneurs wait for sufficient evidence to feel safe before acting, only **11.2%** of those with more than $50 million in revenue do. The wealthiest entrepreneurs have built a "courage advantage"—**28.1%** embrace significant risks as essential (versus 22.1% overall), and significantly more jump on big ideas immediately (**23.6%** versus **16.1%** overall).

When your heart races before a big decision, the 94.6% call it anxiety. The 5.4% call it activation.

PAUL ABEL: WHEN EVERYTHING YOU BUILD GETS DESTROYED (AND YOU BUILD ANYWAY)

Paul Abel knows the fear you're feeling at 2:47 A.M. But his wasn't about one decision—it was about betting his family's home on a vision nobody else could see.

THE $40,000 WAKE-UP CALL

Running 12 successful bagel shops in San Diego should have been enough. But when an employee accident brought OSHA to his commissary, Abel discovered something that would reshape his life: He was fined $40,000 for compliance failures he didn't even know existed.

"We could handle the fine," Abel recalls. "But I kept thinking about tiny businesses with few resources. This could destroy them overnight."

While the 94.6% would have paid the fine and moved on, Abel saw something different. The real fear wasn't the fine—it was that millions of small businesses were one inspection away from disaster.

"There was no OSHA store or one-stop place to go for all the things a business needs regarding compliance," he says. "I saw a need that wasn't being met."

THE COURAGE TO LOSE EVERYTHING FIRST

No bank would loan money to a bagel shop owner to start a compliance company. Abel faced the decision that defines the 5.4%:

"We sold our home. My wife, our two kids—ages three and six—and I went from having our own rooms to sharing space and living off fold-up plastic tables. I was 40 years old with $130,000 and a limited runway to succeed."

This is greater courage: not the absence of fear but the willingness to lose everything material to gain everything meaningful.

THE COURAGE CASCADE IN ACTION

Abel's journey exemplifies how the 5.4% systematize courage through cascading breakthroughs:

Step 1: Name the fear. "I was terrified of failing my family after selling our home." Naming it stripped away its power. Fear thrives in vagueness; it dies in specificity.

Step 2: Reframe as opportunity. "What if this compliance gap wasn't a nice-to-have but a must-solve problem?" Every fear hides an opportunity of equal magnitude.

Step 3: Act immediately. He leveraged relationships with buyers at major retailers and secured shelf space—first 18 months profit: $800,000. Speed defeats hesitation. Momentum murders doubt.

Step 4: Learn from failure. Then came 2008. The recession hit. His major retailer eliminated the entire office supply department. Revenue went to $0 overnight.

"Perfect," Abel could have said sarcastically. But instead, he thought, "Now I know retail dependency is a vulnerability. What's next?"

Step 5: Compound the leap. Each destruction became a bigger reconstruction.

Second Reinvention (2011–2015):

- Partners with 300+ business associations
- Builds online compliance empire
- Becomes #1 on Google for compliance
- *Then, disaster:* SEO firm's tactics get the site blocked
- Revenue vanishes again; broke for the second time

Third Reinvention (2016–2023):

- Partners with HR firms and payroll companies
- Creates subscription model—*like McAfee preinstalled on Dell*
- Builds to 200,000+ subscribers
- 19 firms compete to acquire
- Exits for multiple millions

"I had a mission to simplify compliance to help employers avoid fines and lawsuits," Abel explains. "That's what motivated me for 16 years. If your mission is to make a billion dollars, you're going to give up when the alligators and snakes come out. It's that bigger purpose that gives you the courage you need to keep going."

The Abel Principle: Courage isn't the absence of fear. It's having a purpose bigger than your fear.

HOWARD SCHULTZ: THE 242 REJECTIONS THAT BUILT A $97 BILLION EMPIRE

While Abel discovered courage through destruction, Howard Schultz learned it through rejection — 242 times.

THE TERROR NOBODY UNDERSTOOD

Schultz wanted to buy Starbucks — then 11 stores in Seattle — for $3.8 million. His vision seemed insane to investors: Transform coffee from a commodity Americans bought at gas stations into a premium experience they'd pay $3 for.

"I heard every conceivable reason why my idea would fail. Americans won't pay that much for coffee. You can't compete with Folgers. Coffee shops are where old men read newspapers, not where communities gather."

He approached 242 people. 217 said no. His wife was pregnant with their first child. They had no income. But Schultz had discovered what Abel learned through destruction: When everyone says impossible, fear is pointing toward inevitability.

THE GREATER COURAGE FRAMEWORK IN PRACTICE

Schultz didn't just persist — he architected courage through five transformative principles:

Courage to grow: Each rejection made him refine the vision, not abandon it

Obstacles as raw material: Americans won't pay $3? Create an experience worth $5. Can't compete with Folgers? Don't — create a new category

Constantly innovating: From coffee to food. From stores to mobile apps. From transactions to experiences

Your up-front future: A public commitment turns the fear of failure into fuel for achievement

Courage breeds courage: When the team saw him get rejected 242 times and keep going, they stopped fearing failure. Courage is contagious. So is fear. You choose which spreads

THE $97 BILLION VALIDATION

What systematic courage created:

- **1987:** 11 stores, $3.8 million purchase price
- **1992:** ~165 stores, IPO at $17/share

- **2008:** Nearly 17,000 stores despite recession fears
- **2025:** 40,000+ stores, $97 billion market cap at year-end

The fundamental transformation was cultural. Schultz didn't just build coffee shops — he created "third places" bridging work and home. He didn't just sell coffee — he sold connection.

Three times Schultz left and returned to Starbucks. Each return required more courage than the last:

- **2008:** Returned during the recession, closed 900 stores, retrained 135,000 baristas
- **2022:** Returned at age 69 to transform the company again

Courage, Schultz has long maintained, isn't a one-time event. It's a daily choice to face your fears rather than flee from them.

JENSEN HUANG: WHEN EVERYONE SAYS YOUR VISION IS STUPID

While Abel rebuilt from destruction and Schultz persisted through rejection, Jensen Huang discovered courage by betting everything on a future only he could see — and nearly losing it all three times.

THE GRAPHICS CARD GRAVEYARD

Huang co-founded NVIDIA with Chris Malachowsky and Curtis Priem with a terrifying vision: Graphics would become as important as computing itself. The industry laughed. Graphics cards were for games. Real computing happened on CPUs.

They were told repeatedly they were building toys. Intel dominated computing. Why would anyone need specialized graphics processors?

By 1996, NVIDIA was 30 days from bankruptcy. They had the wrong architecture. Competitors were winning. Employees were leaving.

THE FIRST COURAGE TEST: PIVOT OR PERISH

The board wanted safer markets. The venture capitalists wanted to sell. The team wanted to stabilize. Huang chose terror: rebuild everything from scratch. New architecture. New vision. Bigger bet.

He told the team they had two choices: die slowly doing what was safe, or possibly die quickly doing what was right. But if they survived the second path, they'd change computing forever.

THE CUDA COMMITMENT

NVIDIA was finally successful in gaming—$3 billion in revenue, stable, profitable, safe. That's when Huang made the decision that almost destroyed everything: to invest more than $1 billion—nearly all the company's profits—into CUDA, a platform enabling developers to use graphics chips for general-purpose computing. Over the following decade, the total investment would reach $12 billion.

For five years, CUDA generated virtually zero revenue. Wall Street punished the stock. The board questioned his sanity. Employees wondered whether gaming success had made him delusional. Everyone could see the cost. Almost nobody could see the future.

THE THIRD NEAR-DEATH: BETTING ON AI BEFORE AI

Still investing heavily in CUDA. Gaming competitors were catching up. The stock was stagnant. Huang doubled down: NVIDIA was now an AI company.

The response was brutal: AI is academic fantasy. Nobody needs that much computing power. Stick to games. Huang's answer: In 10 years, everything will be AI. We're building the infrastructure for a world that doesn't exist yet.

THE $4.6 TRILLION VALIDATION

What betting on an invisible future created:

- **1993:** Founded at a Denny's, 30 days from bankruptcy by 1996
- **2006:** $3 billion revenue—committed $12 billion to CUDA over a decade
- **2012:** $4 billion market cap; AI researchers discover NVIDIA GPUs are perfect for deep learning
- **2020:** Every major AI breakthrough runs on NVIDIA
- **2023:** ChatGPT explodes—all on NVIDIA hardware
- **2025:** $4.6 trillion market cap at the close of 2025—larger than most countries' GDP

The most significant risk, Huang has long argued, isn't betting on the future. It's optimizing the present.

THE PSYCHOLOGY OF THE 5.4%: WHY FEAR IS YOUR FRIEND

Dan Sullivan learned through bankruptcy that comfort is the enemy of growth. John Bowen discovered through a family business collapse that the "safe" path is often the riskiest. Both rebuilt by running toward fear, not away from it.

Neuroscience reveals why the 5.4% seek fear.

THE TERROR-TO-TRIUMPH CIRCUIT

When you face something terrifying:

1. Amygdala activates (fight/flight/freeze)
2. Prefrontal cortex engages (executive function)
3. Hippocampus becomes involved (memory formation)
4. Dopamine releases upon action (reward reinforcement)

The 94.6% stop at Step 1. The 5.4% complete the circuit.

Abel completed this circuit three times—each business destruction activated fuller engagement. Schultz completed it 242 times—each rejection strengthened his neural pathways for courage. Huang completed it through a decade of bleeding money—each year of losses deepened his conviction.

Every time you choose courage over comfort, you literally rewire your brain to seek bigger challenges. Fear becomes fuel. Terror becomes triumph.

THE AI AMPLIFICATION OF COURAGE

By 2027, AI will be able to handle all operational tasks. The only remaining human advantage? The courage to pursue what AI cannot imagine.

AI can't:

- Feel fear and choose to proceed anyway
- Sell a house to fund a vision (Abel)
- Persist through 242 human rejections (Schultz)
- Bet a profitable company on an invisible future (Huang)

But AI can amplify your courage by

- Tracking patterns in your fear responses
- Identifying when fear correlates with opportunity
- Reminding you of past courageous victories
- Automating operations so you can focus on courage-requiring decisions

Huang's bet on AI computing created the infrastructure that makes AI possible. His courage literally enabled the technology that now amplifies courage for everyone else.

The 5.4% use AI to handle everything that doesn't require courage, freeing them to focus entirely on what does.

THE HIDDEN COST OF COMFORT

That $180 million acquisition offer on your desk? Let's calculate the real cost of taking it.

The Immediate Gain:

- $180 million pretax
- Eliminate business risk
- Secure generational wealth
- Finally "relax"

The Invisible Loss:

- The $2 billion company you'd build in 10 years
- The industry transformation you'd lead
- The thousands of jobs you'd create
- The legacy that would outlast you by decades

Abel could have stopped after his first success—$800,000 profit seemed like enough. His courage to continue led to 200,000 subscribers and a multimillion-dollar exit.

Schultz could have stopped after one store succeeded. His courage to expand built a $97 billion company that transformed global culture.

Huang could have stayed in a gaming company. His courage to bleed money for a decade built an empire that powers the AI revolution with a $4.6 trillion market cap at the close of 2025.

The brutal truth: Every comfortable exit is an uncomfortable ending to what could have been.

THE COURAGE MULTIPLICATION SYSTEM

The 5.4% don't just feel courage—they systematize it through five multiplying practices.

Practice 1: Fear harvesting. Start a fear journal. Every Sunday, write three things that terrify you about the coming week. By Friday, attempt at least one.

Abel's journal might have had these entries:

- "What if I can't feed my family after selling our house?"
- "What if the compliance market doesn't exist?"
- "What if I fail again after Google destroyed us?"

Each fear faced became fuel for the next.

Practice 2: The 10% Edge Protocol. Continuously operate 10% beyond your comfort zone. Not 50% (burnout), not 5.4% (stagnation)—precisely 10% (optimal growth).

- **Schultz's Rule:** "Each store should scare us a little. If opening it feels easy, we're not pushing hard enough."
- **Huang's Version:** "Every year, bet 10% more on the invisible future."

Practice 3: The Failure Festival. A monthly celebration of productive failures. The biggest failure gets the biggest reward.

Abel could have had three massive celebrations—each business destruction taught him something crucial for the next iteration.

Practice 4: Public Declaration. Announce your scary goal before you know how to achieve it. A public commitment transforms the fear of failure into fuel for innovation.

Huang told the world that NVIDIA would power AI, even though AI barely existed at the time.

Practice 5: Courage Partnerships. Partner with someone whose courage compounds yours.

Abel partnered with associations and payroll companies that weren't afraid of disrupting compliance. Schultz partnered with investors who finally saw his vision. Huang partnered with AI researchers who shared his belief in an invisible future.

Your 25-year vision isn't waiting for you to feel ready. It's waiting for you to feel afraid—and do it anyway.

THE FINAL CALCULATION

You've reached the end of the Greater Game Pyramid. You've built the foundation for freedom, generated energy for expansion, mastered collaboration and multiplication, and now stand at the peak of exponential impact.

Ambition gave you the vision. Security gave you the foundation. Motivation gave you the energy. Property gave you the assets. The community gave you the ecosystem. Teamwork gave you the leverage. Autonomy gave you the freedom. Agency gave you the market. Commitment gave you the persistence.

Now courage gives you the activation energy to transform everything.

It's 4:47 A.M. now. The acquisition offer is still on your desk: $180 million.

But the calculation has changed. It's no longer about the money you gain versus the money you risk. It's about the person you become versus the person you abandon.

Paul Abel sold his house. Howard Schultz faced 242 rejections. Jensen Huang bet everything on an invisible future.

They chose terror over comfort. They chose calling over cash. They decided on the Greater Game.

Now it's your turn.

Pick up the phone. Say no to the offer. Say yes to your vision.

And run toward the roar.

THE BRIDGE: FROM COURAGE TO CATALYST

You stand at the precipice of a life-defining decision—the choice between securing immediate wealth and pursuing your 25-year vision. You've realized the paralyzing truth: You're not afraid of failing; you're terrified of playing small.

The 94.6% see fear as a stop sign. They prioritize comfort over calling, seeking safety and certainty before acting. They take the safe exit, choosing immediate gain while sacrificing exponential future growth. They confuse the absence of risk with the presence of success.

The 5.4%, like Paul Abel, Howard Schultz, and Jensen Huang, understand that fear is a compass. They don't seek to eliminate terror; they transform it into fuel. They know that the same neural pathways that process fear also process excitement. They run toward the roar, recognizing that the most significant risk isn't betting on the future but optimizing the present. Greater commitment gives you the persistence to stay the course; greater courage gives you the daring to leap when the path demands it.

It's time to stop running from fear and start running toward it.

THE MULTIPLIER ACTIVATION: THE FEAR-TO-FUEL REFRAME

This exercise is designed to shift your relationship with fear—from seeing it as a paralyzing force to recognizing it as a signal for activation. It utilizes the neuroscience principle that fear and excitement are nearly identical physiological responses, separated only by your interpretation.

Step 1: Name the Terror (the Specific Fear)

Identify the single most terrifying decision or action you are currently avoiding. Be specific. Vague fear paralyzes; specific fear activates.

- The action that terrifies me: _______________
  ____
  ____
  ____
  ____

- *Examples: Turning down the acquisition offer to pursue the $2 billion vision or betting the company on an unproven technology like Huang did with CUDA.*

Step 2: The Worst-Case Autopsy (the Reality Check)

Define the absolute worst-case scenario if you take this action and it fails. Quantify the impact (financial, reputational, emotional).

- The absolute worst-case outcome: __________

  ____

  ____

  ____

  ____

  ____

- *Example: Paul Abel: "We lose the runway from selling the house. I fail my family and have to start over at 40."*

Step 3: The Capability Gain (the Hidden ROI)

Regardless of the outcome, what new capability, resilience, or strategic insight will you gain simply by attempting this courageous act?

- The capability I will gain: ________________

  ____

  ____

  ____

- *Example: The resilience to handle massive rejection (Schultz); the strategic insight from testing a market that doesn't exist yet.*

Step 4: The Reframe (from Fear to Fuel)

Reinterpret the physical sensation of fear (racing heart, tight chest) not as anxiety, but as activation—your body preparing for a breakthrough. Write your new interpretation of this fear.

- My fear is actually: ______________________

  ____

  ____

  ____

  ____

  ____

  ____

  ____

- *Example: "This terror is the activation energy required to launch my 25-year vision."*

The Scorecard: Measure Your Courage

Quantify your current capacity to transform fear into fuel. Score yourself from 1 (fear avoidant) to 12 (fear seeking) in each category:

Category	Description	Now (1–12)	12-Month Target
Fear Recognition	I see fear as data and a compass, not danger.	___	___
Opportunity Reframing	I systematically transform fears into possibilities and fuel.	___	___
Action Velocity	I act decisively and quickly, even in the face of uncertainty and discomfort.	___	___
Failure Harvesting	I view failure as a stepping-stone and systematically learn from setbacks.	___	___
The 10% Edge Protocol	I continuously operate 10% beyond my comfort zone.	___	___
Public Declaration	I announce scary goals before I know how to achieve them.	___	___
Courage Cascade	My courageous actions inspire and multiply courage in others.	___	___
TOTAL SCORE:		___ / 84	

Score Interpretation:

- **7–35:** Fear is controlling you (the 94.6% trap; prioritizing comfort).
- **36–60:** You are beginning to transform fear (developing courage systems).
- **61–84:** Fear is your fuel (the 5.4% zone; unstoppable).

THE DASHBOARD INTEGRATION: ACTIVATE YOUR COURAGE

Your Fear-to-Fuel Reframe and Scorecard are the final inputs into your Greater Game architecture. You have all 10 multipliers. Now please activate them.

Go to TheGreaterGameDashboard.com and input your Greater Courage score.

Here's how the platform catalyzes your transformation:

1. **The Courage Benchmark:** Compare your score against the 39.3% of $50+ million entrepreneurs who actively treat failure as fuel for their most significant breakthroughs—versus the majority who wait for certainty—as tracked by the Entrepreneurial Pulse.
2. **The Command Center View:** Your Greater Courage score is the final metric, completing your greater multipliers index (GMI). View your comprehensive profile and see your readiness for the 100x future.
3. **Your Recommended Actions:** Based on your complete Greater Game architecture, the platform surfaces personalized pathways:

- VFO Second Opinion—If your fears center on wealth preservation, concentration risk, or financial complexity, this pathway transforms anxiety into architecture.
- Strategic Coach Acceleration—If your fears involve operational dependency, team limitations, or scaling challenges, this pathway provides the courage frameworks to act decisively.

The most significant risk isn't losing what you have; it's never becoming who you could be. Fear is your compass. Activate your dashboard and start your Greater Game now.

CONCLUSION

YOUR GREATER GAME BEGINS NOW

The 5.4% don't have better opportunities—they have better architecture. You now have the blueprint.

5:47 A.M.—THE SAME BED, A DIFFERENT CALCULATION

You're in the same beautiful home. But this time it's dawn, and you're not staring at the ceiling, paralyzed by the 2:47 A.M. exhaustion of optimization.

You're sitting at the edge of the bed with a notebook, energized by the clarity of architecture.

The same $20 million business, the same 60 employees—but where you once saw operational bottlenecks and endless effort, you now see 10 multipliers waiting to be activated.

You came to this book having won the 94.6% game—a game of linear growth, zero-sum competition, and sacrificial effort. You discovered the realization that destroys most successful entrepreneurs: You hadn't misplayed the game; you had outgrown the field.

The exhaustion wasn't burnout. It was misalignment. It was the sound of your multipliers trying to break through.

Your 14-year-old daughter's question from the Introduction still echoes: "What exactly do you do that's so important you miss my games?"

But now you have an answer that will make both of you proud.

THE RECOGNITION THAT CHANGES EVERYTHING: 100X IS EASIER THAN 2X

You now understand the central paradox that defines the 5.4%.

When you aim for 2x, you optimize. You fight the physics of your current model. It's exhausting.

When you aim for 100x, optimization is impossible. You are forced to architect something entirely new. You build platforms, ecosystems, and intellectual property. This architectural approach requires less effort over time because the systems scale up automatically.

Dan's bankruptcy and John's family collapse proved that optimization without architecture eventually fails. Success built on effort is fragile. Success built on multipliers is invincible.

You have made the crucial shift: from expert to architect, from operator to creator.

THE COMPLETE ARCHITECTURE: THE PYRAMID REALIZED

You have traversed the four stages of the Greater Game Pyramid. You haven't just learned 10 concepts; you have integrated an exponential operating system.

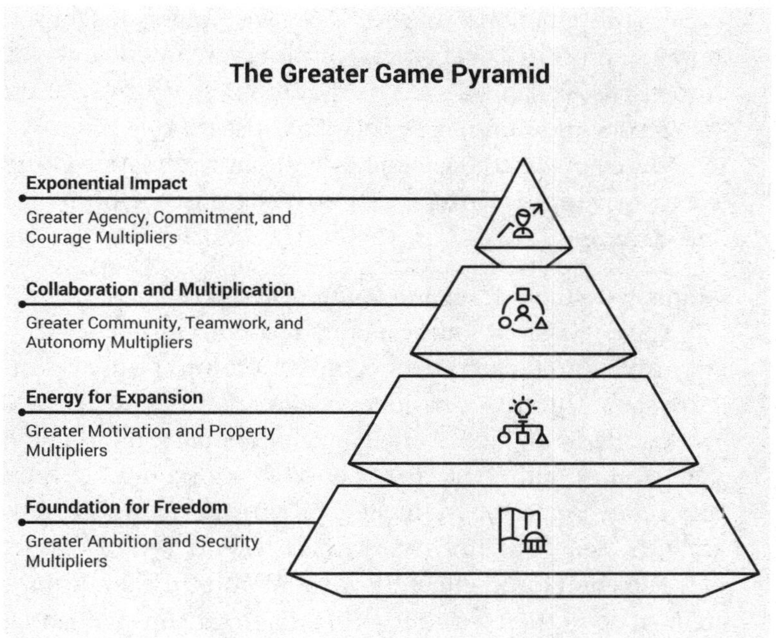

Stage 1: Foundation for Freedom

You established your launchpad. Greater ambition shifted your horizon from quarterly results to a 25-year vision. Greater security permitted you to execute that vision fearlessly, transforming the "VFO gap" (fragmented advice) into orchestrated invincibility.

The compound effect: Vision without a fortress is vulnerability; security without vision is stagnation. Together, they create the foundation for fearless execution.

Stage 2: Energy for Expansion

You built your engine. Greater motivation shifted you from the depletion cycle of external validation to the generation cycle of the "emotional paycheck." Greater property taught you how to capture that energy, transforming your invisible genius into visible, scalable IP—assets that multiply your valuation (15–30x) while eliminating the "expertise trap."

The compound effect: Energy without systematic capture is expensive enthusiasm. Together, they transform brilliance into an empire.

Stage 3: Collaboration and Multiplication

You engineered your scale and freedom. Greater community transformed zero-sum competition into positive-sum ecosystems through "free-zone collaborations." Greater teamwork shifted your focus from managing people to multiplying genius, eliminating the "indispensability discount." Greater autonomy made you invincible, proving the "absence multiplier"—that your business grows faster when you are gone.

The compound effect: IP without an ecosystem is limited; an ecosystem without self-managing teams is chaotic. Together, they create exponential scale and true freedom.

Stage 4: Exponential Impact

You became the architect of the future. Greater agency empowered you to stop reacting to markets and start creating them through category design. Greater commitment provided the strategic stubbornness to persist when others pivot. Greater courage taught you to use fear as your compass, transforming terror into fuel.

The compound effect: Creation without commitment is experimentation; commitment without courage is determination without daring. Together, they achieve revolutionary transformation.

THE COST OF INACTION: THE 18-MONTH WINDOW IS NOW

The three forces introduced at the beginning of this journey—AI commoditization, the $124 trillion wealth transfer, and the category creation premium—are accelerating. The 18-month window is closing. Optimization is no longer a viable strategy.

You now face three possible futures.

Future A: The Optimization Trap (the 94.6% Default)

You return to the 2:47 A.M. calculations. You work harder within the existing constraints. You optimize your way to irrelevance as AI automates your advantages and category creators redefine your industry. You exit for 3–5x EBITDA, exhausted and constrained.

Future B: The Partial Implementation (the Dangerous Middle)

You cherry-pick a few comfortable multipliers. You achieve temporary improvement followed by more profound exhaustion. Like John's family foundry, you have perfect systems without transformation. The collapse is delayed, not avoided.

Future C: The Full Architecture (the 5.4% Commitment)

You activate all 10 multipliers systematically. You shift from optimization to architecture. You build ecosystems, IP, and self-managing teams. You command 15–30x valuation multiples. You achieve exponential impact and true freedom.

THE SYSTEM IS THE SOLUTION: ACTIVATE YOUR DASHBOARD

The 5.4% don't rely on willpower; they rely on systems. The Greater Game Dashboard is the system for your transformation.

Scan the QR code at the conclusion of the book or go to TheGreaterGameDashboard.com and input your scores from all 10 chapters.

This activates your personalized Command Center:

1. **Your GMI (Greater Multipliers Index):** See your comprehensive profile and your readiness for the 100x future.
2. **The Entrepreneurial Pulse Benchmark:** Compare your scores against the top 5.4% of performers tracked in our monthly research.
3. **Your Recommended Actions:** Based on your complete GMI profile, the platform surfaces personalized pathways:
    - **VFO Second Opinion**—If your scores reveal wealth complexity, concentration risk, or security gaps, this pathway provides capital alignment and coordinated advisory solutions.

- **Strategic Coach Acceleration**—If your scores reveal gaps in implementation, operational frameworks, or autonomy, this pathway provides the execution systems to close them.

Don't just read about transformation—systematize it.

YOUR PERSONALIZED 90-DAY SPRINT

Your dashboard doesn't just show you where you are—it shows you where to start.

Based on your GMI profile, your Command Center prioritizes the specific multipliers that will create the greatest leverage for your unique situation. The exercises from each chapter are your toolkit.

Stage	Your Toolkit
Foundation for Freedom	100x Architecture Draft, Invincibility Audit
Energy for Expansion	Energy Audit, 20-Minute IP Capture
Collaboration and Multiplication	Competitor-to-Collaborator Shift, Empowerment Inversion, 48-Hour Disappearance Test
Exponential Impact	Category Design Challenge, Strategic Stubbornness Matrix, Fear-to-Fuel Reframe

Your recommended actions tell you which tools to pick up first. The dashboard adapts as you progress—what matters most today may shift as your architecture evolves.

A LETTER FROM YOUR FUTURE SELF

Before you choose your path, imagine receiving this:

Thank you.

Thank you for choosing architecture over optimization that morning. Thank you for recognizing that the 2:47 A.M. exhaustion wasn't a life sentence, but a signal for transformation.

Thank you for refusing to accept the indispensability discount. Thank you for responding to our daughter's question with action, not just words.

Everything that matters in my life today—the industry we transformed, the ecosystems we built, the family memories we created, the legacy that outlasts us—all started with your decision to play the Greater Game.

You could have taken the safe path. You could have sold for "enough." You could have continued the cycle of exhaustion.

Instead, you chose to multiply. And that choice didn't just change your business—it changed everything.

—Your future self

THE MONDAY MORNING REVOLUTION

This Monday is different. Not because your business changed overnight—but because your architecture for it has transformed.

7:00 A.M.: architecting your 25-year vision, not checking e-mails

9:00 A.M.: empowering leaders (greater teamwork), not managing people

11:00 A.M.: designing new categories (greater agency), not optimizing operations

Noon: lunch with your family—present, energized, invincible

YOUR DAUGHTER'S QUESTION, ANSWERED

"What exactly do you do that's so important?"

"I'm architecting an ecosystem that will outlast me by generations. I'm transforming an entire industry by creating new categories. I'm building systems that multiply impact without multiplying effort. And starting today, I'm doing it in a way that includes you, not excludes you. Want to help me design what comes next?"

THE FOUNDER DECLARATION: SIGN THIS

- **To yourself:** *"I will not optimize my way to exhaustion. I will architect my way to exponential impact."*

_____________________________ Date: __________

- **To your future:** *"I commit to the 100x vision, recognizing that 100x is easier than 2x."*

_____________________________ Date: __________

- **To your legacy:** *"I will build systems that multiply without me and create a legacy worth telling."*

_____________________________ Date: __________

WELCOME TO THE 5.4%

That 2:47 A.M. exhaustion that opened this book? It wasn't a problem. It was your genius trying to evolve.

The 18-month window? It's not closing—it's opening wider for those with the architecture to leverage it.

You came looking for your next level. You found your next game entirely.

The 94.6% will close this book and return to optimization.

The 5.4% will close this book and activate their architecture.

The Greater Game doesn't start tomorrow. It starts now.

The most significant transformations start with systematic clarity.

Activate Your Command Center

Scan the QR code or go to TheGreaterGameDashboard.com.

The following 25 years begin today.

ACKNOWLEDGMENTS

From Dan and John

This book exists because of the 25,000+ entrepreneurs we've had the privilege of working with over the past five decades. You taught us everything we know about the Greater Game. Your willingness to share your struggles, breakthroughs, and hard-won wisdom made this book possible.

To the entrepreneurs who opened their stories for these pages—Scott Akerley, Jennifer Borislow, Roderick Walker, Paul VanDuyne, Jonathan Cotten, Homer Smith, Nate Brown, Mike Wandler, Dale Wills, Steven Neuner, Gino Wickman, Keegan Caldwell, John Kissell, Saša Krcmar, David Reiling, Kent Pilcher, Evan Ryan, Beth Kraszewski, Mark Young, Carter Froelich, Jerry Browder, Paul Abel, Joe Polish, and many others. . .

To Kary Oberbrunner, whose strategic vision shaped not just this book but also how it will reach the entrepreneurs who need it most—thank you for helping us think bigger about the launch.

To our teams: The Strategic Coach family has spent 35+ years refining the frameworks in this book. Shannon Waller, Cathy Davis, and the entire Toronto team—your dedication to entrepreneur transformation is unmatched.

To Melody Guy and the Hay House team—thank you for believing that entrepreneurs deserve a book that challenges them to play a bigger game.

From Dan

To Babs Smith, my partner in life and business—you've been my greatest multiplier for over four decades. Everything I've built, I've built with you.

To John Bowen—our collaboration proves the thesis of this book. Two architects working together create something neither could alone.

To Becca Miller, my assistant—your tireless support behind the scenes made this book possible.

From John

To Dan Sullivan—you transformed how I think about entrepreneurship, and this book is the culmination of 17 years of learning from you.

To Jeanne, my wife—your love and support through every chapter of our life together has made everything possible.

To the top financial advisors I've had the privilege of working with—you dedicate your careers to serving entrepreneurs, and your commitment to excellence inspires this work every day.

To the CEG Elevate Group team who made this book possible: Heather O'Donnell, our COO, whose hands touched every part of this project from start to finish. Robin Black, our Managing Principal of Strategic Relationships, who saw the need for this book before anyone else. Paul Lofties, who leads VFO Connect and understood how bringing together top financial advisors and successful entrepreneurs creates tremendous value. George Walper and Cathy McBreen, and the CEG Insights team—your research captured the essence of who entrepreneurs are and what they truly need. And Mark Klimek, who worked directly with the entrepreneurs to capture each of their stories. This book stands on the foundation you built.

To Marissa Sparks, my assistant, who coordinated everyone and everything throughout this entire project—your patience and precision kept us all on track.

To every entrepreneur who picks up this book at 2:47 A.M., wondering if there's a bigger game—there is. Welcome to it.

ABOUT THE AUTHORS

DAN SULLIVAN is the world's foremost expert on entrepreneurship and the co-founder of Strategic Coach®, the world's leading entrepreneurial coaching program. Over the past 50 years, he has worked personally with more than 25,000 entrepreneurs, helping them achieve exponential growth while gaining freedom from the day-to-day operations of their businesses.

Dan is the author of more than 50 publications, including the bestselling books *The Gap and The Gain*, *Who Not How*, and *10x Is Easier Than 2x*. His frameworks—including Unique Ability®, Free Days, and the Self-Managing Company—have become foundational concepts in entrepreneurial thinking worldwide.

Dan lives in Toronto with his wife and business partner, Babs Smith.

JOHN BOWEN is the founder and CEO of CEG Elevate Group, which helps the world's top financial advisors deliver exceptional value to entrepreneurial clients through the Virtual Family Office (VFO) model. His research through CEG Insights has surveyed thousands of entrepreneurs, producing the Greater Multipliers Study and Entrepreneurial Pulse research cited throughout this book.

A 17-year member of Strategic Coach, John has authored or co-authored more than 20 books on wealth management and entrepreneurial success. He has been recognized as one of the most influential figures in the financial services industry and is a sought-after speaker on entrepreneurial wealth strategies.

John lives in San Martin, California, with his wife of 45 years, Jeanne.

Together, Dan and John have spent decades studying what separates the top 5.4% of entrepreneurs from the rest. *The Greater Game* is their first book together—but not their last. Consider it your invitation to join them.

We hope you enjoyed this Hay House book. If you'd like to receive our online catalog featuring additional information on Hay House books and products, or if you'd like to find out more about the Hay Foundation, please contact:

Hay House LLC, P.O. Box 5100, Carlsbad, CA 92018-5100
(760) 431-7695 or (800) 654-5126
www.hayhouse.com® • www.hayfoundation.org

Published in Australia by:
Hay House Australia Publishing Pty Ltd
18/36 Ralph St., Alexandria NSW 2015
Phone: +61 (02) 9669 4299
www.hayhouse.com.au

Published in the United Kingdom by:
Hay House UK Ltd
1st Floor, Crawford Corner,
91–93 Baker Street, London W1U 6QQ
Phone: +44 (0)20 3927 7290
www.hayhouse.co.uk

Published in India by:
Hay House Publishers (India) Pvt Ltd
Muskaan Complex, Plot No. 3,
B-2, Vasant Kunj, New Delhi 110 070
Phone: +91 11 41761620
www.hayhouse.co.in